DOCTOR'S FIX: ♥
HEART-SMART DIABETICS:

Step by Step Freedom Plan

Your Journey
from Dis-ease to Wellness

DR SUKHBINDAR SINGH SIBIA
DR HARPREET KAUR SIBIA
World famous No-surgery
Heart Traeatment Pioneers

BlueRose ONE.com
Stories Matter
NewDelhi • London

BLUEROSE PUBLISHERS
India | U.K.

BlueRose ONE.com
Stories Matter
NewDelhi • London

For permissions requests or inquiries about this publication, please contact:

BLUEROSE PUBLISHERS
www.BlueRoseONE.com
info@bluerosepublishers.com
+91 8882 898 898
+4407342408967

ISBN: 978-93-7018-652-1

Cover design: Yash Singhal
Typesetting: Namrata Saini

First Edition: May 2025

This book weaves together practical advice, scientific insights,

and a light dose of humor to keep the readers engaging.

It emphasizes the role of the Glycemic Index (GI),

Continuous Glucose Monitoring (CGM),

and lifestyle modifications,

while offering actionable steps

toward reversing Type 2 diabetes.

Dedicated To

To every person who has ever felt overwhelmed by the burden of diabetes but refused to give up.

To the families and friends who stand by their loved ones, offering support, love, and encouragement on the journey to better health.

To the healthcare professionals and coaches who inspire hope and empower individuals to reclaim their lives.

And most importantly, to you, the reader—who is brave enough to believe in change, strong enough to take the first step, and committed enough to create a life free from limitations.

This book is for you. May it be the guide and companion you need to discover the power you already have within.

Together, we reverse. Together, we thrive.

Foreword

Type 2 diabetes has long been viewed as a chronic, irreversible condition—one that demands lifelong management with medications, strict diets, and constant vigilance. But what if I told you that diabetes doesn't have to be a life sentence? What if the future could look different—free from glucose spikes, pills, injections, and worries about complications? This book is here to show you that it is possible.

The power to reverse diabetes is no longer a far-off dream. Science, research, and real-life success stories prove that with the right lifestyle changes—combined with commitment, consistency, and a touch of humor—you can take control of your health and even achieve complete remission. What you'll find in these pages is not just another guide on managing diabetes; it's a playbook for reversing it.

The author takes a refreshingly practical, compassionate, and motivational approach, laying out step-by-step strategies that work in the real world. This is not about deprivation or harsh discipline. It's about learning how your body works, making smart food choices, staying active, and managing stress without sacrificing the joy of living. What makes this book special is the way it speaks to both the science and the heart of reversing diabetes, with easy-to-follow advice, tools, and encouragement every step of the way.

Why This Book Matters Now

The burden of diabetes in modern society is heavier than ever. Millions of people worldwide live with Type 2 diabetes, and many more are on the verge of diagnosis. Beyond the numbers, the disease takes a silent toll—the emotional strain of worrying about complications, the frustration of juggling medications, and the fear of losing control over your health.

But times are changing, and so is our understanding of diabetes. Research now shows that reversal is possible, especially when action is taken early. The challenge, though, lies in navigating the overwhelming amount of information, advice, and myths that surround diabetes care. That's where this book comes in—cutting through the noise with clear, actionable guidance based on science and real-life success stories.

The Role of Coaching, Community, and Support

One of the most inspiring messages in this book is the importance of not doing it alone. Changing habits can feel challenging, especially if you've been managing diabetes for years. But coaching and community support can make all the difference. Whether it's a group of friends and family members going through the same journey or a personal coach to keep you accountable and motivated, having someone by your side ensures that you stay on track when life throws inevitable challenges your way.

In this book, the author emphasizes that diabetes reversal is not just an individual pursuit that can be done with loved ones, friends, or even entire communities. When families eat healthier together, when friends hold each other accountable, and when groups share their victories, the impact goes far beyond individual success. Health becomes a shared journey.

A Roadmap to Transformation

The author takes a holistic, empowering approach, integrating the latest knowledge about nutrition, exercise, fasting, stress management, and glucose monitoring. From practical meal plans based on Indian cuisine to time-restricted eating routines and mindful stress reduction techniques, every chapter offers simple but powerful tools to make sustainable lifestyle changes.

This book does something rare, it not only educates but also motivates. It recognizes that real change takes time and that everyone needs a little push now and then. It encourages you to celebrate small wins, embrace progress over perfection, and stay consistent even when the going gets tough.

Your Journey Starts Here

This book is more than just a guide; it's an invitation—to take charge of your health, to believe in your ability to reverse diabetes, and to create a future that's vibrant, joyful, and free from the limitations of chronic illness. If you're ready to change your life, this book will walk with you every step of the way—offering encouragement, practical tools, and a clear path forward.

As you read these pages, remember: You're not alone on this journey. Whether you're at the beginning of your reversal plan or well on your way, you have the support, knowledge, and tools to succeed. Believe in yourself. The future you've dreamed of—a life full of health, energy, and freedom—is within your reach.

A Final Thought

Diabetes doesn't define you. You define your story—and this book is your guide to writing a new chapter, one filled with health, hope, and joy. Your journey begins now, and I can't wait to see all that you achieve.

Turn the page. Your new life awaits.

With gratitude, encouragement, and excitement for your journey ahead,

Dr Nikhil Gupta, MD

Preface

When exploring the idea of reversing Type 2 diabetes, we encounter a common belief - that once diagnosed, diabetes is a lifelong condition to be managed, not reversed. But as we dug deeper, we discovered that this doesn't have to be true. In fact, countless individuals, with the right approach, have regained control of their health, reduced or eliminated medications, and now enjoy a life free from the complications that often accompany diabetes. This book is born from that realization - a belief that reversal is not only possible but achievable with practical tools, knowledge, and determination.

The goal of this book is to offer a new perspective on diabetes management, shifting the narrative from one of lifelong struggles to one of empowerment and hope. The authors have created a roadmap for those seeking freedom from diabetes - a guide that not only informs but also motivates and supports individuals every step of the way.

Why This Book

This book isn't just about lowering blood sugar, it's about transforming your life. Diabetes affects more than just your body, it touches your emotions, relationships, and the way you experience everyday life. Doctors understand that the road to reversing diabetes isn't always easy, but it is easier when you don't try to do it alone. Many people feel isolated or overwhelmed by the process, and that is why this book emphasizes coaching, community, and family support as key components of success.

The strategies shared in these pages, whether it is about time-restricted eating, personalized coaching, practical meal planning, or managing stress, are designed to fit into real life. This book is as much about sustainable change as it is about achieving short-term goals. The mission is to help build habits that last, not just for a few months but for the rest of your life.

Who is This Book For

This book is for anyone living with Type 2 diabetes or prediabetes, whether you have recently been diagnosed or have been managing it for years. It is also for those who want to reduce or eliminate their dependence on medications and those looking to avoid complications like heart disease, nerve damage, kidney issues, etc.

Even if you do not have diabetes yourself, you are not prediabetic on alert or do not have a strong positive family history of diabetes, this book can be a powerful resource if you are supporting a loved one on their journey. Whether you are a spouse, parent, friend, or caregiver, your involvement makes an enormous difference. When families and communities come together to adopt healthier habits, everyone benefits. Remember all present Type II diabetics were normal at one time.

The Approach: Simple, Practical, Empowering

Throughout this book, you will find real-world advice grounded in science and practical experience. The authors have broken down complex medical concepts into easy-to-understand language and provided step-by-step strategies that can fit into your daily routine—no matter how busy life gets. From tracking your progress with a CGM to building low-GI Indian meals, each chapter is filled with actionable tools to make your journey smoother and more enjoyable.

But beyond practical advice, this book is also filled with encouragement and humor. Reversing diabetes is a serious goal, but that does not mean it has to be all work and no joy. Celebrating small wins, laughing through the challenges, and reminding ourselves that progress is more important than perfection.

Your Takeaway

My hope is that this book gives you the confidence to believe in your own power. Reversing diabetes is not about deprivation, it is about taking back control and building a lifestyle that works for you. Some days will feel easy, and others will be tough, but always remember that every step forward matters.

This book is not just a guide, but it is an invitation to reimagine what's possible for your health and your life. It is a reminder that you are not your diagnosis, and that small, consistent actions have the power to create profound change.

A Note on Coaching and Community

One of the recurring themes in this book is the importance of coaching and community support. Even the most motivated individuals need help staying on track sometimes. Whether it is personalized coaching, group sessions with family and friends, or online support communities, having someone on your corner makes all the difference. We are stronger together, and sharing the journey with others brings motivation, accountability, and joy.

A Personal Call to Action

If you have picked up this book, it means you are ready to make a change—and that is a powerful step. The author's call to action for you is simple: Do not wait. Start now. The tools, knowledge, and strategies in these pages are here to help you take control of your health today. And you do not have to do it alone — this book will be with you every step of the way, cheering you on and helping you navigate the challenges.

The journey to reversing diabetes is not about perfection, it is about progress, persistence, and staying motivated even when the path feels tough. Be confident that with the right mindset, practical tools, and support system, you can transform your health and your life.

Trusr yourself in this journey. Now, get started—and create the future you deserve.

With hope, encouragement, and belief in your potential,

Dr Keerat Kaur Sibia, MD

Acknowledgements

Authoring this book has been a journey in itself—one filled with learning, inspiration, and countless moments of gratitude. It would not have been possible without the support, encouragement, and guidance of many people along the way.

Primarily, to the readers, thank you for trusting me to be part of your journey toward reversing diabetes. Your commitment to reclaiming your health is the driving force behind this book. Every story of success, every small win, and every step you take forward inspires me. This book is written for you, and because of you.

To my family and friends, who have been my rock throughout this process. Thank you for your love, patience, and constant encouragement. Your belief in me made this book possible.

To the healthcare professionals, nutritionists, fitness trainers, and diabetes educators who are working tirelessly to change lives, thank you for your dedication and the invaluable insights you have shared. Your work serves as the foundation for many of the principles in this book.

To the individuals who shared their success stories and allowed me to feature their journeys, thank you for your openness and courage. Your stories remind us that reversing diabetes is not only possible but achievable.

To the coaches, mentors, and accountability partners who guided me along the way—thank you for teaching me the importance of staying motivated, connected, and focused on progress, not perfection. Your wisdom and support shaped many of the ideas in this book.

To my editorial team and publishing partners, thank you for your hard work, patience, and creativity. Your diligence and belief in this project ensured that this book became a reality.

And finally, to every person who has struggled with diabetes and chosen to fight back—thank you for your resilience. Your efforts and determination are a testament to the human spirit, and your victories are a beacon of hope for others.

This book is a product of the love, guidance, and shared wisdom of all these people—and for that, I am deeply grateful.

With heartfelt thanks,

Dr Harpeet Kaur Sibia

Director: Sibia Medical Centre

Introduction

Reversing Diabetes – A Journey Back to Health

Imagine waking up every morning full of energy, without the worry of checking blood sugar levels or remembering to take medications. Picture yourself free from the constant fear of diabetes-related complications, enjoy life with the people you love, and know that you are in control of your health. This is not a dream, it is entirely possible, and you are holding the blueprint to make it happen in your hands.

Welcome to Reversing Diabetes

A Journey Back to Health. This book is not about temporary fixes, crash diets, or quick hacks. It is about understanding the root causes of Type 2 diabetes and making lasting, practical changes that put you back in the driver's seat. Whether you have been recently diagnosed with or have been managing diabetes for years, this book will show you that reversal is within reach - and yes, it can even be enjoyable.

What You will Discover in This Book

In these pages, we will dive deep into the science behind diabetes - how it develops, what goes wrong inside the body, and most importantly, how to reverse the damage and regain control. But this is not just another health guide filled with jargon and rules. It is packed with practical strategies that fit into your lifestyle, no matter where you are or how busy life gets.

Here is what you can expect:

- Clear explanations of how blood sugar, insulin, and metabolism work.
- Tools like CGM (Continuous Glucose Monitoring) help you track your progress in real time.
- Easy, low-GI meal plans tailored to Indian cuisine, along with tips for enjoying regional foods without spiking your blood sugar.
- Timing and portion size of meals.
- Exercise routines that fit into your day, whether you prefer walking, yoga, or strength training.
- Stress management techniques that help you stay calm, focused, and in control.
- Real-life success stories from people who have reversed their diabetes.
- Guidance on how to collaborate with your doctor to safely reduce or eliminate medications.
- Motivational coaching tools to keep you on track, even when things get tough.

Who is This Book For

This book is for anyone who:

- Has Type 2 diabetes and is ready to take control of their health.
- Wants to prevent complications like heart disease, nerve damage, or kidney issues.
- Feels overwhelmed by medications and seeks a way to reduce or eliminate them.

- Is tired of feeling stuck and needs practical, actionable steps to create lasting change.
- Cares about their family and friends and wants to build a healthier environment for everyone.
- Prediabetics on diet control may not cross the border.
- Those with positive family history.

It is also for those who may not have diabetes themselves but support loved ones on their health journey. The information in this book can benefit entire families, helping everyone adopt healthier habits that last a lifetime.

Why This Book is Different

There is no shortage of advice on diabetes, but too much of it feels rigid, overwhelming, or outdated. This book takes a different approach—it is designed to be practical, positive, and empowering. It is about small, sustainable changes that create big results.

I believe that reversing diabetes does not mean giving up on the things you love, it is about making smarter choices, finding joy in the process, and staying motivated through every step of the journey. That is why you will find this book filled with real-world tips, humor, and encouragement.

The Promise of Reversal: Yes, You Can Do This

The medical community is increasingly recognizing that Type 2 diabetes is not a one-way street—it can be reversed. Many people who once believed they would spend their lives managing diabetes are now living proof that it is possible to bring blood sugar back to normal levels and reduce or eliminate medications. The earlier you start, the easier the reversal—but it is never too late to make a change.

This journey will not be perfect. There will be setbacks and challenges along the way, but that is normal. You do not have to be perfect to make progress. The important thing is to keep going, one step at a time. With the right tools, knowledge, and support, you can regain control, transform your health, and reclaim your life.

Let Us Get Started – Your Journey Begins Now

This book isn't just about information, it's call to action. It is your chance to take control of your health, break free from the limitations of diabetes, and live the vibrant, active life you deserve.

Whether you are looking for motivation to take the first step or guidance to fine-tune your habits, you will find what you need here. Together, we will explore how small, sustainable changes can lead to big, lasting transformations. You will learn how to outsmart your glucose levels, move your body with joy, and enjoy delicious meals without compromising your health.

Are you ready to begin? Your new life starts now. It is time to take control, reverse diabetes, and build a future filled with health, energy, and joy. Let us take this journey together—because the best is yet to come.

Turn the page and let us get started.

Dr Ilmjot Singh Sibia

CEO: Sibia Medical Centre

Contents

Chapter 1
Introduction – Reversal is Possible (Oh! Really!)

You have just heard it, haven't you? "Once a diabetic, always a diabetic." Pffft! Let me tell you the upfront: That is as outdated as bell-bottom jeans. With the right game plan, Type 2 diabetes is not a life sentence, it is more like an annoying house guest who can be kicked out.

Reversing diabetes is not some miracle cure; it is science—simple, solid, sugar-slaying science. This book is for those who are ready to give their pancreas a standing ovation by putting glucose back in its place, after a prolonged period of insult by overburdening your pancreas or forcing it to start a protest in the form of Type II diabetes. It is practical, it is doable, and yes, you might even laugh along the way. After all, humor is one of the healthiest sugars out there—and it is 100% glycemic index free.

So, you have been diagnosed with Type 2 diabetes, and you are thinking, "Well, this is it. No more sweets, endless medications, and finger pricks for life." That is what the internet or, worse, your nosy aunt has told you. But let me start this book with a bold claim: Diabetes can be reversed. And I am not talking about some magic pills or internet swindles involving exotic berries. We are talking science-backed, practical changes that can put your blood sugar back in its place—*permanently*.

If you have been told that diabetes is a one-way street, it is time to turn that GPS around. With the right tools, you can not only reduce or eliminate medications, but you can also get your A1C levels (the three-month blood sugar average) back to normal. This chapter sets the stage for the rest of the book, helping you understand what "reversal" really means and how you can achieve it. Spoiler alert: You are going to outsmart your pancreas and have fun doing it.

The Big Myth: Can Diabetes Actually Be Reversed?

The short answer: Yes.

The long answer: Yes—but it takes effort, patience, and some smart lifestyle changes.

Reversing diabetes does not mean you get to eat cake for breakfast again, but it does mean that your body can heal. Specifically, reversal refers to bringing your blood sugar levels back to non-diabetic ranges without needing medication. If your fasting glucose and A1C readings stay normal over time, congratulations—you have kicked diabetes to the curb.

Now, there is a catch: Reversal is easier the sooner you catch the problem. The longer your body stays in a high-sugar state, the harder it gets to undo the damage. But even if you have been battling this condition for years, there's hope—and this book is here to show you how.

Type 2 Diabetes: Not a Death Sentence, just a Speed Bump

Let us get one thing clear—Type 2 diabetes is not your fault. It is not because you ate one too many donuts (although, yes, that did not help). A combination of genetics, lifestyle, and environment creates the perfect storm for insulin resistance. But here is the good news: If lifestyle causes it, lifestyle can fix it.

Think of your pancreas as an overworked employee at a donut factory. It is doing its best to manage all the sugar being thrown at it, but eventually, it gets tired, sluggish, and overwhelmed. Our job is to give your pancreas a break, train your cells to be more insulin-sensitive, and reduce glucose levels naturally.

What Reversal Looks Like (And What It Does not)

Before we dive in, let us define what success looks like in the context of diabetes reversal:

- Normal fasting glucose: Below 100 mg/dL
- A1C below 5.7%
- No need for medications to manage blood sugar.

Now, what it *does not* mean is that you can go back to an all-you-can-eat carb fest. Maintenance is key, but do not worry, we will cover how to indulge safely without derailing your progress.

Think of diabetes reversal as running a marathon, not a sprint. There will be times when you want to give up. But by the time we are done, you will know how to manage slip ups, setbacks, and even the occasional slice of pizza without guilt.

What Makes Reversal Possible? A Peek Behind the Science

Here is a little secret: Your body wants to heal. It is designed to be a fine-tuned machine, and when we remove the obstacles (excess sugar, insulin resistance, belly fat), it can repair itself surprisingly well.

The science of diabetes reversal is based on these key principles:

1. Improving Insulin Sensitivity: Insulin is like a key, unlocking your cells so glucose can enter. In Type 2 diabetes, the key stops working because the lock (your cells) gets rusty. By losing excess fat and eating smarter, we can "lubricate" the lock and restore your cells' sensitivity to insulin.
2. Burning Through Glucose Reserves: With every bite you take, glucose enters your bloodstream. Your liver stores extra glucose like a pantry storing snacks. If you stop eating frequently or switch to time-restricted eating, your body burns through these glucose reserves, helping restore blood sugar balance.
3. Weight Loss Reduces Insulin Resistance: Belly fat (also known as visceral fat) releases chemicals that interfere with insulin function. When you lose weight—especially around your waist—your cells become more responsive to insulin, making it easier to control glucose levels.
4. Your Secret Weapon: The Glycemic Index (GI) Foods with a low glycemic index release glucose slowly, giving your pancreas time to manage it. High-GI foods are the culprits behind glucose spikes. You will learn how to swap out the offenders and build meals that keep your blood sugar rock steady.

A Sneak Peek at What is to Come

Throughout this book, we will walk you through every step of diabetes reversal. It is not about starving yourself or spending hours in the gym. We are focusing on sustainable changes, trivial things that have an enormous impact. Here is what to expect:

- You will become best friends with your glucose monitor. It is not scary; it is just feedback.
- You will learn how to "game" your meals using the glycemic index.
- Fasting and time-restricted eating will become part of your toolkit.
- Exercise will become your glucose-burning secret weapon (and no, it will not involve burpees unless you like them).

And here is the best part: We are going to have fun doing this. If there is one thing we know for sure, it is that humor and joy make the hard stuff a lot easier. You will laugh, you will learn, and you might even start enjoying broccoli (no promises, though).

Common Questions You Might Have at This Point

Q: Is diabetes reversal the same as a cure?

A: Think of it more as remission. If you go back to old habits, the condition can return. The goal is to stay in control, just like brushing your teeth daily to avoid cavities.

Q: How long will it take to reverse my diabetes?

A: It varies. Some people see dramatic improvements in a few months, while others take a bit longer. It depends on how consistently you follow the strategies in this book.

Q: Will I need to give up all my favorite foods?

A: Not entirely! Moderation and smart swaps are the names of the game. We will show you how to indulge without spiking your glucose.

Q: What if I mess up?

A: You will. And that is okay. Progress is not linear, and slip-ups are part of the process. The key is getting back on track without guilt.

Let Us Get Started!

Now that you know reversal is not just possible but doable, it is time to roll up your sleeves and dive in. Each chapter will build on the last, giving you the tools, knowledge, and confidence to take control of your blood sugar and your life.

Ready to outsmart your glucose and turn this ship around? Let us start —your pancreas will thank you later. And remember: If life hands you lemons... squeeze them into a low-GI smoothie.

This introduction sets a positive, practical tone for the book, making it clear that diabetes reversal is both possible and sustainable. The humorous, easy-going style aims to keep readers engaged while building excitement for the actionable advice to come.

Chapter 2
Diabetes Demystified – What's Happening in Your Body?

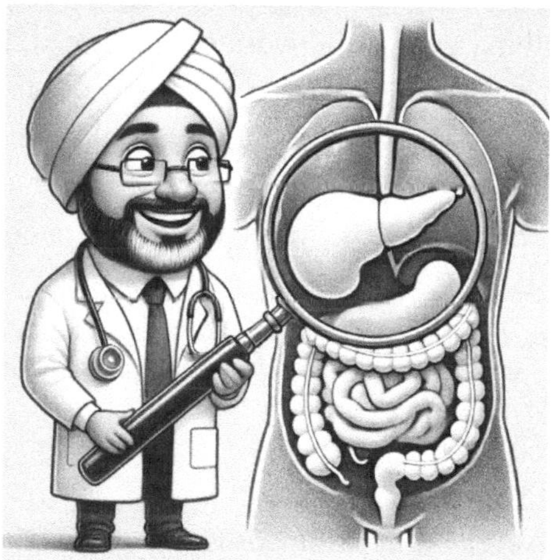

Let us break it down:

Diabetes is your body saying, "Hey, I'm having trouble managing all this sugar!" Normally, your pancreas releases insulin, the hormone that tells your cells, "Open up, food's here!" But in Type 2 diabetes, your cells give insulin the cold shoulder—like a teenager ignoring curfew calls. This leads to insulin resistance and high blood sugar levels.

The good news? Just like a cranky teen, insulin resistance can be won over—with the right care, attention, and snacks (more on that later).

Let us kick things off with the basics—what exactly is Type 2 diabetes, and why is your body acting like it is confused about sugar? In this chapter, we will decode the science behind diabetes in plain English, helping you understand what is going wrong and what we can fix. Spoiler alert: Your body is not broken—it just needs a little reboot. So, let us dig in with a dose of humor to keep things light.

How Glucose is Supposed to Work (When All Goes Well)

Imagine your body as a car, and glucose (sugar) as fuel. Every time you eat something with carbohydrates (like bread, rice, or fruit), your body converts it into glucose. That glucose flows into your bloodstream, and your pancreas releases insulin, which acts like a valet. Insulin's job is to open the "gates" of your muscle, fat, and liver cells, letting the glucose inside to burn as energy or store as fat for later use.

In a healthy system, the sequence goes something like this:

1. You eat.
2. Glucose enters your bloodstream.
3. Your pancreas sends out insulin.
4. The glucose gets stored or burned, and your blood sugar stays within a normal range.

Smooth, right? But what happens in Type 2 diabetes? The system breaks down, and glucose ends up overstaying its welcome in the bloodstream. Let us look at where things go off the rails.

What Goes Wrong in Type 2 Diabetes?

The real villain here is insulin resistance. Over time, especially if you are eating too many high-GI foods or carrying extra weight, your cells become resistant to insulin's efforts. It is like someone knocking on your door with dinner, but you refuse to answer because you have been eating too much junk lately. The glucose has nowhere to go and builds up in the bloodstream, causing high blood sugar levels.

The pancreas, trying its best, keeps pumping out more insulin to get the job done. But eventually, it gets exhausted—like a tired waiter working double shifts—and cannot keep up. This is when your blood sugar levels remain high consistently, leading to Type 2 diabetes.

The Two Key Problems in Type 2 Diabetes

1. Insulin Resistance:
   - Your cells stop listening to insulin, so glucose cannot enter.
   - This leaves too much sugar floating in your bloodstream.

2. Beta-Cell Burnout:
   - Your pancreas gets overworked trying to produce more insulin.
   - Over time, your beta cells (the insulin-producing cells) lose their ability to function properly.

If untreated, these two problems compound over time. Elevated blood sugar can start to damage your eyes, kidneys, nerves, and heart—turning you into a walking science experiment. But that is where we come in to reverse the process.

Symptoms of Type 2 Diabetes: What to Watch For

In many cases, diabetes sneaks up on people. Some folks walk around for years without knowing they have it, only realizing after a random blood test. But if you are noticing these symptoms, it is time to pay attention:

- Excessive thirst: You feel parched no matter how much water you drink.
- Frequent urination: It is like you have become best friends with the bathroom.
- Fatigue: You feel drained, even after a full night's sleep.
- Blurred vision: Your eyes get fuzzy, making reading menus impossible.
- Slow-healing wounds: Your cuts and scrapes seem to take forever to heal.
- Tingling in hands and feet: Your nerves are not happy with high blood sugar levels.

These are signs that your body is struggling to regulate glucose, and if you catch it early enough, you can reverse the damage before it gets worse.

How Sugar Becomes the Problem Child

Eating sugar is not the enemy—poor glucose management is. Carbohydrates are essential because they provide the energy you need to get through the day. However, the problem lies in the type and amount of carbs you consume.

- Simple carbs (high GI): White bread, sugary drinks, pastries—these carbs hit your bloodstream like a sugar tsunami, spiking glucose levels.
- Complex carbs (low GI): Vegetables, whole grains, and legumes release glucose slowly, giving your body time to process it.

When you are constantly eating high-GI foods, your pancreas never gets a break. It is stuck working overtime, and soon enough, your insulin system is out of order.

Fat and Insulin Resistance: The Belly Fat Connection

Let us talk about belly fat, or as I like to call it, the "VIP lounge for insulin resistance." Visceral fat—the fat around your organs—produces chemicals that interfere with insulin's work. It is like a bunch of bouncers at a nightclub, keeping insulin from doing its job.

Studies show that losing even 5-10% of your body weight can significantly improve insulin sensitivity. That is why weight loss is often the first step in reversing diabetes. But do not worry, we are not aiming for a six-pack here. Even minor changes can make an enormous difference.

What Happens If You Do Not Act? The Risks of Untreated Diabetes

If diabetes is not managed, it can lead to some serious complications. Think of these as the fines you pay for ignoring glucose.

- Heart disease: High blood sugar damages blood vessels, increasing your risk of heart attacks.
- Kidney damage: Elevated glucose levels strain your kidneys, potentially leading to kidney failure.
- Eye problems: Diabetic retinopathy can cause blindness if untreated.
- Nerve damage: Neuropathy makes it hard to feel your feet, increasing the risk of infections and amputations.

The goal here is not to scare you, it is to empower you to act before these complications arise. With the strategies in this book, you will be equipped to stop diabetes in its tracks and avoid these risks altogether.

Good News: Your Body Wants to Heal

The human body is amazing. It is designed to repair and regenerate, and even with Type 2 diabetes, it is not too late to start healing. Research shows that with the right combination of diet, exercise, and glucose monitoring, many people can reverse diabetes symptoms and return to non-diabetic blood sugar levels. Your pancreas might need a little encouragement, but it is far from retired.

Why You are in the Driver's Seat

Here is the key takeaway: You are in control. While genetics and family history play a role, most Type 2 diabetes cases are related to modifiable lifestyle factors. This means that by making smart food choices, exercising regularly, managing stress, and using glucose monitors effectively, you can reverse the condition.

The best part? Small steps lead to big results. You do not have to overhaul your life overnight, just a few changes, practiced consistently, can get you on the path to reversal.

Action Steps to Take Right Now

Before we dive into the practical details in later chapters, here are some things you can start doing today:

1. Check your blood sugar levels: If you have not done so already, ask your doctor for an A1C test.
2. Start tracking your meals: Write down what you eat, it will help you spot hidden sugar culprits.
3. Move a little every day: A 10-minute walk after meals can reduce glucose spikes.
4. Cut out sugary drinks: Swap sodas for water or herbal teas.

5. Measure your waist: Track your progress as you lose belly fat—it is a major step toward reversal.

Closing Thoughts: You've Got This

Now that you understand what is happening inside your body, it is time to take control. Diabetes is not a life sentence—it is just a challenge. And challenges are meant to be overcome. In the next chapters, we will dive into practical strategies that will not only lower your blood sugar but also help you enjoy the journey.

Remember: You are not your diagnosis. You are someone with the power to turn things around—and it starts right now.

Ready to outsmart glucose? Let us move on to the next chapter and learn about the sneaky ways food affects your blood sugar. You will be amazed at how easy it can be to make smarter choices once you know the science behind it.

This chapter builds the foundation for readers, giving them the knowledge they need to understand what is happening in their bodies and setting the stage for the practical strategies that follow. The tone is encouraging and empowering, emphasizing that diabetes is manageable and reversible with the right approach.

Chapter 3
Meet the Villains – Glycemic Index, Glycemic Load, and Hidden Sugars

Understanding Glycemic Index (GI): Your Food's Sugar Score

The Glycemic Index (GI) is like a movie rating for carbs. A low GI means "boring documentary" (think leafy greens), while a high GI is "action thriller" (white bread, we are looking at you). The lower the GI, the slower your food turns into sugar, which means fewer glucose spikes and a happier pancreas.

Here is a quick cheat sheet:

- Low GI (below 55): Lentils, chickpeas, leafy greens
- Medium GI (56-69): Sweet potatoes, quinoa

- High GI (70+): White rice, doughnuts, and yes, sadly, mangoes

But wait, there is more! Glycemic Load (GL) adjusts for portion size, so you are not vilifying one bite of banana. A low-GI food in truckloads is still trouble.

All right, buckle up—it is time to introduce the sneaky troublemakers that have been quietly wreaking havoc on your blood sugar: Glycemic Index (GI), Glycemic Load (GL), and hidden sugars. Understanding these villains will be key to managing and eventually reversing your diabetes. The good news? Once you learn how to spot them, you will know how to beat them at their own game. This chapter is your backstage pass to the secret lives of carbs.

The Glycemic Index (GI): The Sugar Speedometer

The Glycemic Index (GI) is like a speedometer for your food, it measures how quickly carbohydrates in a food raise your blood sugar. Foods are given a score between 0 and 100, with pure glucose scoring one hundred (the Usain Bolt of sugars).

- Low GI (55 or less): These foods release sugar slowly, keeping your glucose levels steady. Think of lentils, leafy greens, and chickpeas.
- Medium GI (56-69): These foods cause moderate rises in blood sugar. Sweet potatoes and basmati rice are in this category.
- High GI (70+): These foods are like fireworks—instant sugar bombs. White bread, sugary cereals, and watermelon belong here.

Why should you care?

When you eat high-GI foods, they cause spikes in your blood sugar, which makes your pancreas pump out a ton of insulin to keep things under control. Over time, this constant insulin surge makes your cells resistant, leading to diabetes.

The Trouble with Spikes: Rollercoasters Are Not Fun for Your Glucose

Think of your blood sugar levels like a rollercoaster. High-GI foods make the rollercoaster go up and down dramatically, leaving you feeling tired, hungry, and irritable. And just like with a real rollercoaster, the more you ride it, the worse you feel by the end of the day. Stable glucose levels = happy pancreas + happy you.

This is why choosing low-GI foods is a game-changer in diabetes reversal. They keep your glucose levels steady, prevent cravings, and reduce the workload on your pancreas.

Glycemic Load (GL): GI's Smarter Cousin

While Glycemic Index (GI) measures the speed of sugar release, Glycemic Load (GL) factors in how much carbohydrate there is in the portion you are eating. This makes GL a more practical guide for real-world eating.

Here is an example:

- Watermelon has a high GI (80), but a low GL (around 5). Why? Because a typical serving of watermelon does not contain much carbohydrate.
- Bagels have both a high GI and high GL, making them double whammy.

Formula for Glycemic Load (GL):

The Glycemic Load (GL) formula is calculated by multiplying the Glycemic Index (GI) of a food by the amount of available carbohydrates in a serving and then divided by 100:

GL = (GI x grams of carbohydrate per serving) / 100

- Low GL: 10 or less
- Medium GL: 11-19
- High GL: 20 or more

So, what is the takeaway? Small portions of high-GI foods may not be as harmful as substantial portions. This is why portion control matters as much as food choice.

How to Use GI and GL in Everyday Life

Here is a straightforward way to apply GI and GL principles:

- Swap white rice with brown rice or quinoa (lower GI).
- Choose whole fruits over fruit juices (lower GI and more fiber).
- Go for small portions of carbs paired with healthy fats (like nuts or avocado), which slow down glucose absorption.

These small swaps add up and will make a significant difference to your blood sugar levels over time. And remember—this is not about cutting carbs completely. It is about choosing the right carbs and eating them smartly.

Hidden Sugars: The Sneaky Saboteurs

Just when you thought you had a handle on things, hidden sugars show up. Food manufacturers are experts in disguise, slipping sugar into places you would never expect—like ketchup, salad dressings, and even "healthy" granola bars. They use fancy names like maltodextrin, agave syrup, dextrose, and fructose to trick you.

Here is a quick cheat sheet:

- Any word ending in " ose" = Sugar (glucose, fructose, sucrose)

- Corn syrup, malt syrup = Avoid these at all costs
- "Natural" sweeteners like agave = Still sugar, just with better marketing

Tip: Always check food labels for "Total Carbohydrates" and "Added Sugars". Even foods labeled “low-fat” or “healthy” can be loaded with sugar to compensate for the lack of flavor.

The Glycemic Index Does Not Tell the Whole Story

While GI and GL are powerful tools, they are not perfect. Some foods with low GI, like chocolate or ice cream, are still unhealthy if eaten in excess (high fat and calories). Similarly, high-GI foods like potatoes can be healthy in lesser amounts, especially if eaten with fiber-rich vegetables or protein.

The key is balance—pair your carbs with fiber, protein, or healthy fats to keep your glucose levels from spiking. For example:

- Add avocado to your toast to lower the GI impact.
- Pair fruit with nuts to slow down sugar absorption.

How Stress, Sleep, and Exercise Influence Glycemic Response

Food is not the only factor affecting your blood sugar. Stress, lack of sleep, and sedentary behavior can all raise your glucose levels, even if you are eating well. High cortisol levels (the stress hormone) interfere with insulin sensitivity, making it harder for your cells to absorb glucose.

Quick tips:

- Manage stress with yoga, meditation, or deep breathing exercises.
- Get at least 7-8 hours of sleep to reduce glucose fluctuations.

- Moving after meals, a 15-minute walk can significantly reduce post-meal spikes.

Practical Strategies for Low-GI Living

To make GI and GL work for you, here is a handy list of smart substitutions:

- Breakfast: Swap sugary cereals for steel-cut oats topped with chia seeds and berries.
- Lunch: Replace white bread sandwiches with whole grain wraps or lettuce wraps.
- Dinner: Choose sweet potatoes over regular fries and brown rice over white.
- Snacks: Keep nuts, seeds, or Greek yogurt handy instead of chips or cookies.

And remember: It is not just what you eat, but how you eat. Eating slowly and chewing thoroughly improves digestion and reduces glucose spikes.

Debunking Common Myths About Carbs and Sugar

1. Myth: All carbs are bad.
   Truth: Complex, low-GI carbs are essential for energy and overall health.

2. Myth: Honey and agave are better than sugar.
   Truth: All sugars, no matter how natural, affect blood glucose levels.

3. Myth: You need to avoid fruits.
   Truth: Whole fruits are packed with fiber, which slows glucose absorption—just do not overdo it.

Your GI & GL Toolbox: Making Informed Choices

Here is a quick summary of foods to favor and foods to limit based on their GI and GL:

Low-GI Foods (Good Choices):

- Lentils, chickpeas, beans
- Vegetables (except starchy ones like potatoes)
- Whole grains (quinoa, barley)
- Berries, apples, pears

High-GI Foods (Limit or Avoid):

- White bread, white rice
- Sugary cereals, candy
- Soft drinks, fruit juices
- Potatoes (unless eaten in moderation with fiber and fats)

A Word of Encouragement: You are in Control.

Mastering the Glycemic Index and Glycemic Load is not rocket science, it is about making smarter choices. Once you start eating low-GI foods consistently, you will notice your blood sugar levels stabilize, your energy improves, and your cravings decrease. You are not giving up food you love, you are just learning how to enjoy it without sending your glucose on a rollercoaster ride.

In the next chapter, we will introduce you to one of the coolest tools in your reversal journey: Continuous Glucose Monitoring (CGM). It is like having a personal detective tracking your blood sugar levels 24/7. You are going to love how empowering it feels to finally understand your body's response to food in real time.

So, let us wrap up the villain talk for now—because you have the upper hand. Ready to become a glucose ninja? Let us dive into the next chapter and learn how to outsmart your blood sugar, one data point at a time.

Chapter 4
CCG – Continuous Glucose Monitoring: Your Glucose Detective

HbA1C – is it important or Random Blood Sugar versus Fasting Blood Sugar versus Glucose Tolerance Test

Forget those quarterly blood sugar reports—CCG gives you real-time scoop. It is like having a detective on your side, always checking in on how your meals, workouts, and even stress are affecting your glucose levels.

With CCG, you will learn that oatmeal is not as innocent as it seems (if you dump honey), and that a 10-minute walk after a meal can do wonders to flatten that post-dinner spike.

Welcome to the world of Continuous Glucose Monitoring (CGM), where blood sugar monitoring goes high-tech! CGM is like having your own personal detective on the job, constantly tracking and reporting what your glucose is up to 24/7. It is not just a toolkit; it is a game-changer in the world of diabetes management and reversal. In this chapter, we will explore how CGMs work, why they are essential for reversing diabetes, and how you can use this technology to stay a step ahead of sneaky glucose spikes.

What Is a Continuous Glucose Monitor (CGM)?

Forget the old-fashioned finger pricks that give you just a snapshot of your blood sugar at one moment in time. A CGM gives you continuous real-time data, showing how your glucose levels rise, fall, and stabilize throughout the day and night.

A typical CGM system includes:

1. A tiny sensor inserted just under your skin (usually on your arm or abdomen).
2. A transmitter attached to the sensor, which sends glucose data to a device or app.
3. A mobile app or receiver that shows your glucose trends in real time.

How CGMs Work: Monitoring Glucose Non-Stop

The CGM sensor measures glucose levels in your interstitial fluid (the fluid between your cells) every 5 to 15 minutes. It sends this data to your smartphone or receiver, which displays your current glucose level and a graph showing how it has changed over the past hours. Think of it as a health tracker for your blood sugar.

Bonus: Some CGM systems come with alerts—they will buzz you if your glucose goes too high or too low, so you can act immediately. No more guessing games!

Why CGM is a Game-Changer for Reversing Diabetes

CGM transforms the way you manage diabetes because it provides immediate feedback. With traditional blood glucose meters, you test once or twice a day—but you miss the important story in between. CGM helps you:

- Identify patterns: You will see how specific foods, stress, and exercise impact your glucose levels.
- Catch spikes early: No more waiting for quarterly blood tests. If food raises your glucose too much, you will know right away.
- Make smarter choices: With real-time data, you can tweak meals and activities to keep glucose levels steady.

CGMs give you powerful insights that allow you to fine-tune your diet, exercise, and lifestyle choices—making diabetes reversal much more achievable.

How to Use CGM to Reverse Diabetes: Practical Tips

Here is how you can make the most out of CGM technology:

1. Log your meals and activities: Use a simple notebook or an app to record what you eat, when you exercise, and how you feel. You will start seeing patterns between your habits and glucose levels.

2. Check your glucose before and after meals: Pay attention to your pre-meal and post-meal glucose readings (1-2 hours after eating). If a particular food causes a huge spike, swap it for a lower-GI option in the future.

3. Experiment with exercise timing: Try taking a 15-minute walk after meals and observe how it affects your glucose. Spoiler: It works wonders!

4. Manage stress in real time: Notice if stressful moments cause glucose spikes. If so, use breathing exercises, meditation, or a short walk to bring levels back down.
5. Do not aim for perfection—aim for progress: There will be fluctuations, and that is okay. The goal is to identify trends and make gradual improvements.

Real-Life CGM Insights: The Unexpected Triggers

One of the best things about CGM is that it helps you discover surprising glucose triggers. Here are some real-life examples from CGM users:

- Overnight glucose spikes: Even if you have not eaten anything, stress or poor sleep can raise glucose levels at night.
- Coffee without food: Some people find that black coffee raises their glucose levels, especially on an empty stomach.
- Fasting surprises: During intermittent fasting, some CGM users notice glucose dips that make them feel tired or cranky.
- Fruit's dark side: While whole fruit is healthy, eating too much at once (even low-GI options) can still cause a spike.

These insights are not always intuitive, but with CGM, you get to solve the mystery of your personal glucose responses.

Choosing the Right CGM for You

There are several CGM devices available on the market, each with their own pros and cons. Here are some popular options:

1. Freestyle Libre:
   - Pros: No finger pricks required, budget friendly.

- Cons: Requires scanning to view glucose levels (does not alert you automatically).

2. Dexcom G6:
   - Pros: Provides automatic alerts for highs and lows, integrates with smartwatches.
   - Cons: More expensive than other options.
3. Medtronic Guardian Connect:
   - Pros: Offers predictive alerts to warn of future highs/lows.
   - Cons: Requires calibration with a traditional meter.
4. Gabit
   - Pros: CGM and smart ring integration offers extensive 24/7 health tracking (heart rate, HRV, sleep, etc.) and AI coaching – a major advancement.
   - Cons: Costly one-time upfront fee for the smart ring with CGM integration.

Discuss with your healthcare provider to choose the CGM that fits your needs and budget.

What to Expect When You Start Using CGM

Using CGM is easy, but there is a bit of a learning curve. Here is what you need to know:

- You might feel overwhelmed at first. Do not worry, just focus on the big picture.
- There will be some fluctuations. Glucose is not static, and that is normal.
- It is okay to experiment. Evaluate different meals, workouts, and sleep routines to find what works for you.

The most important thing is to stick with it. Over time, you will get better at interpreting your data and making the right adjustments.

Using CGM with Your Healthcare Team

CGM empowers you to take control of your diabetes, but it is still important to collaborate closely with your doctor or diabetologist. Sharing your CGM data during appointments will give your healthcare team a clearer picture of what's working and what's not. They might also adjust your medications based on your progress.

Bonus tip: Most CGM apps allow you to share your data with your healthcare provider automatically, so you do not have to print anything out.

The Emotional Benefits of CGM: Reducing Fear and Anxiety

Many people with diabetes live in constant fear of unexpected glucose drops or spikes. CGM helps reduce this anxiety by providing real-time insights and eliminating the guesswork. You will feel more confident making decisions about food, exercise, and medications, knowing you have the data to back you up.

And let us face it—knowledge is power. When you understand your glucose patterns, you stop feeling like your body is out of control. Instead, you become the one in charge.

A Day in Life with CGM: What It Looks Like

Here is an example of how CGM can guide your day:

Morning:

- Wake up and check your fasting glucose.
- Have a low-GI breakfast (avocado toast on whole-grain bread).

Lunch:

- Eat grilled chicken with quinoa and veggies. You check your CGM 1 hour later—glucose spike is minimal. Success!

Afternoon:

- You are feeling stressed, and your CGM shows a slight glucose rise. Take a 5-minute walk and watch the levels drop.

Dinner:

- You experiment with sweet potato instead of white rice. Your glucose levels stay steady throughout the evening.

Night:

- Before bed, you check your CGM again—perfect levels to end the day.

This simple day shows how real-time data empowers you to make better choices and stay in control.

The Bottom Line: CGM as Your Personal Diabetes Coach

CGM is more than just a fancy gadget—it is your personal diabetes coach, always on duty, helping you fine-tune your lifestyle for optimal glucose control. Whether it is identifying hidden sugar culprits, testing meal strategies, or adjusting exercise routines, CGM gives you the tools to reverse diabetes faster and smarter.

In the next chapter, we will dive into building your personal diabetes reversal blueprint—combining everything we have learned so far about food, exercise, and glucose monitoring into a practical action plan. Get ready, because with CGM by your side, you are already one step ahead on your journey to reversing diabetes.

Pro Tip: Do not forget to name your CGM system, it is your trusty sidekick now. "Glucose Tracker"? "The Glucose Whisperer"? Whatever makes you smile—because laughter is, after all, the only sugar that is good for you.

CGM indicates HbA1C level and overall success if you are fighting out your spikes and staying in the green zone.

Decoding Diabetes Management: Let us not forget the Traditional Glucose Monitoring

Diabetes management revolves around understanding and controlling blood sugar levels. While traditional methods like HbA1c and various blood sugar tests provide valuable snapshots, Continuous Glucose Monitoring (CGM) offers a revolutionary approach. Let us break down the differences and understand how each tool contributes to the bigger picture.

Traditional Methods:

- **HbA1c:** This blood test reflects your average blood sugar levels over the past 2-3 months. It is like getting a report card for your overall glucose control. A higher HbA1c indicates higher average blood sugar levels and a greater risk of diabetes complications.
- **Fasting Blood Sugar (FBS):** Measured after an overnight fast, this test reveals your baseline glucose level. It helps diagnose diabetes and assess how well your body manages sugar overnight.
- **Random Blood Sugar (RBS):** Taken at any time of day, regardless of meals, this test provides a snapshot of your current blood sugar level. It is useful for detecting

hyperglycemia (high blood sugar) or hypoglycemia (low blood sugar) at a specific moment.

- **Oral Glucose Tolerance Test (OGTT):** This test involves drinking a sugary solution and measuring your blood sugar levels over 2 hours. It assesses how your body processes sugar and is often used to diagnose prediabetes or gestational diabetes.

Continuous Glucose Monitoring (CGM):

CGM uses a small sensor inserted under the skin to continuously measure glucose levels in the interstitial fluid (fluid surrounding cells). This provides real-time data, showing trends and fluctuations throughout the day and night.

CGM Advantages:

- **Comprehensive Picture:** Unlike single-point measurements, CGM provides a dynamic view of how your blood sugar responds to meals, exercise, medication, and stress.
- **Early Warnings:** CGM can alert you to dangerous highs or lows before you experience symptoms, allowing for timely intervention.
- **Personalized Insights:** By revealing patterns and trends, CGM empowers you to make informed decisions about your diet, activity, and medication.
- **Improved HbA1c:** Studies show that CGM use can lead to significant improvements in HbA1c levels.

The Synergy of CGM and Traditional Methods:

While CGM offers a wealth of information, it does not replace traditional methods entirely.

- **HbA1c** remains crucial for long-term assessment and tracking overall diabetes management progress.
- **FBS, RBS, and OGTT** may still be used for diagnostic purposes or when a specific snapshot is needed.

Conclusion:

CGM is a powerful tool that revolutionizes diabetes management by providing real-time insights and empowering individuals to take control of their health.

When used in conjunction with traditional methods, CGM contributes to a comprehensive approach for optimal diabetes care.

Note: Always consult your healthcare provider for personalized advice and guidance on managing your diabetes.

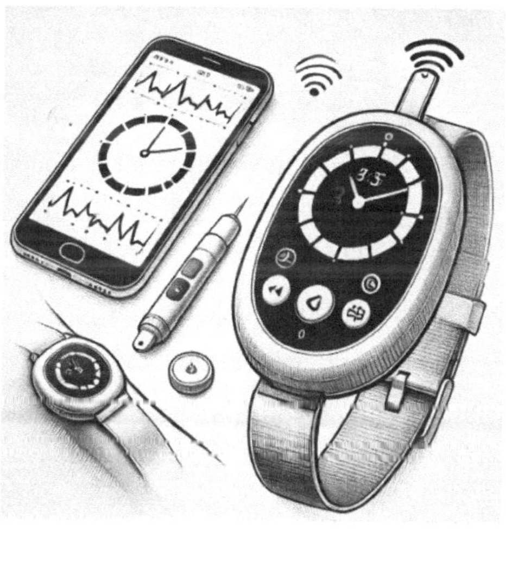

Chapter 5
Building Your Personal Reversal Blueprint

Here is the thing—diabetes reversal is not a one-size-fits-all T-shirt. Your game plan will depend on your diet, routine, medications, and preferences. Together, we will explore:

1. How to identify your "trigger foods."
2. Why carbs are not evil—but they do need supervision?
3. How fasting can be your pancreas' reset button.
4. Creating meals that make your glucose monitor smile.

Welcome to the blueprint for reversing diabetes, customized to fit your life. This chapter is where theory meets action. Just as a tailor makes a suit fit perfectly, your diabetes reversal plan must align with your preferences, routines, and challenges. There's no one-size-fits-all approach here; what works for you might not work for someone else, and that is okay. The goal is to design a sustainable plan that becomes second nature over time.

Think of this blueprint as a step-by-step guide that brings together diet, exercise, glucose monitoring, stress management, and even a bit of fun along the way. Each section will help set achievable goals and personalize your journey toward a healthier, diabetes-free life.

Step 1: Define Your "Why" – Your Personal Motivation

Before you begin, take a moment to answer this: Why do you want to reverse your diabetes?

- To have more energy for your kids or grandkids?
- To reduce or eliminate medications?
- To feel in control of your health?

Your "why" is your North Star. Write it down and refer to it whenever things feel tough, it will keep you motivated when temptation strikes, or progress feels slow.

Step 2: Assess Where You Stand Today

Let us start with a baseline assessment so you know where you are right now. This will help you track progress and adjust your plan as needed.

1. Blood Tests to Know Your Numbers:
    - A1C: Your three-month average blood sugar (aim for below 5.7%).
    - Fasting glucose: A healthy level is below 100 mg/dL.
    - Post-meal glucose: Should be under 140 mg/dL two hours after eating.

2. Measure Your Waistline: Visceral fat is linked to insulin resistance. A waist measurement over forty inches for men and thirty-five inches for women is a risk factor.
3. Log Your Medications: Make a list of the medications you take—your goal is to reduce or eliminate them over time, with your doctor's guidance.
4. Track Your Daily Habits:
    - What does your typical diet look like?
    - How active are you?
    - How often do you feel stressed?
    - What is your sleep schedule?

This assessment will help you identify areas for improvement and shape your plan.

Step 3: Set SMART Goals

Your goals should be SMART—Specific, Measurable, Achievable, Relevant, and Time-bound. Here are some examples:

- Diet: Swap white bread for whole grain bread at lunch every day for 2 weeks.
- Exercise: Walk for 15 minutes after dinner five times a week.
- Stress management: Practice 5 minutes of deep breathing every morning for 30 days.

These small, achievable goals will create momentum and build lasting habits.

Step 4: Create Your Reversal Diet – Personalized Meal Planning

Food is a powerful tool in your diabetes reversal journey. But this is not about deprivation, it is about making smart swaps and loving what you eat. Let us break down your personalized meal plan.

1. Choose Low-GI Foods

Base your meals around foods with a low Glycemic Index (GI) to avoid blood sugar spikes. Here is your cheat sheet:

- Vegetables: Spinach, broccoli, zucchini, bell peppers
- Whole grains: Quinoa, oats, barley, whole wheat
- Proteins: Chicken, fish, tofu, eggs, lentils
- Healthy fats: Avocado, olive oil, nuts, seeds

Tip: Make sure at least half your plate is vegetables, they are low in carbs, full of fiber, and help keep your blood sugar steady.

2. Build Balanced Meals with the Plate Method

The Plate Method is a simple way to build balanced, diabetes-friendly meals:

- ½ plate: Non-starchy vegetables (like greens, broccoli, or cauliflower)
- ¼ plate: Lean proteins (like grilled chicken or tofu)
- ¼ plate: Healthy carbs (like quinoa or sweet potatoes)
- Add healthy fats: Avocado slices or a drizzle of olive oil.

This method ensures a good mix of nutrients that stabilize glucose levels and keep you full.

3. Use Time-Restricted Eating (TRE)

Intermittent fasting or Time-Restricted Eating (TRE) can help your body become more insulin-sensitive. Try eating within an 8-10 hour window each day (e.g., 9 AM to 7 PM) and fasting for the rest. This gives your body time to burn through glucose reserves and improves blood sugar regulation.

Step 5: Incorporate Movement into Your Day

Exercise improves insulin sensitivity and helps burn excess glucose. But do not worry, you do not need to become a marathon runner! Just move consistently.

1. Walking: A 15-30 minute walk after meals can significantly reduce glucose spikes.
2. Strength Training: Building muscle improves insulin sensitivity. Try bodyweight exercises like squats, push-ups, or resistance bands 2-3 times a week.
3. Fun Activities: Dance, swim, or play with your kids—movement does not have to be boring!

Pro Tip: Set a reminder to stand or walk for 5 minutes every hour—it keeps your metabolism active.

Step 6: Monitor Your Progress with CGM and Journaling

Continuous Glucose Monitoring (CGM) is your best friend here. It gives real-time feedback, so you know what is working and what is not. Pair it with a journal to track:

- Meals and glucose responses
- Exercise routines
- Stress levels and sleep patterns.

Use this data to fine-tune your habits. If you notice certain foods cause spikes, swap them out. If stress is raising your glucose, focus on relaxation techniques.

Step 7: Manage Stress and Prioritize Sleep

Stress and sleep play a huge role in insulin sensitivity. Cortisol, the stress hormone, increases blood sugar levels, while poor sleep makes insulin less effective.

Stress Management Techniques:

- Deep breathing: 5-10 minutes of belly breathing can calm your nervous system.
- Yoga or meditation: These practices lower cortisol and improve insulin function.
- Nature walks: Spending time outdoors reduces stress and improves mood.

Sleep Hygiene Tips:

- Stick to a consistent sleep schedule (even on weekends).
- Avoid screens 1 hour before bed—blue light interferes with melatonin.
- Create a relaxing bedtime routine (think reading, journaling, or listening to calming music).

Step 8: Work with Your Doctor and Adjust Medications

Your goal is to reduce or eliminate medications over time, but this must be done in partnership with your doctor. As your blood sugar levels improve, your doctor may lower your doses or stop certain medications.

Warning: Never adjust medications on your own—it is crucial to avoid hypoglycemia (low blood sugar).

Step 9: Track Your Progress and Celebrate Small Wins

Reversing diabetes is a marathon, not a sprint. Along the way, it is important to celebrate your progress, even the small wins.

- Lowered your fasting glucose by a few points? Celebrate with a new workout outfit.
- Stuck to your diet plan for a week? Treat yourself to a movie night (no popcorn!).

These positive reinforcements will keep you motivated to stay on track.

Step 10: Prepare for Setbacks (They Will Happen!)

Let us be real life happens. You might have a difficult day, eat too much pizza, or skip a workout. That is okay. Setbacks are part of the process. The key is to get back on track without guilt.

- Learn from slip-ups: What triggered it? How can you avoid it next time?
- Forgive yourself: Perfection is not required progress is.

Final Thoughts: Building a Life, You Love

This reversal blueprint is not just about managing diabetes, it is about creating a life you love. As you build healthy habits, you will feel more energized, confident, and in control. Remember, you do not have to do everything at once. Start small, stay consistent, and adjust as needed.

In the next chapter, we will dive deeper into low-GI cooking tips, recipes, and meal ideas to keep your taste buds happy while your blood sugar stays steady. You have the blueprint—now let us start building!

Pro Tip: Treat your journey like planting a garden. Some days it will rain, some days it will not—but if you keep tending to it, you will see the fruits of your effort bloom.

Chapter 6
The Food Formula – Low-GI Foods and Smart Substitutions

(With a Focus on Indian Cuisine)

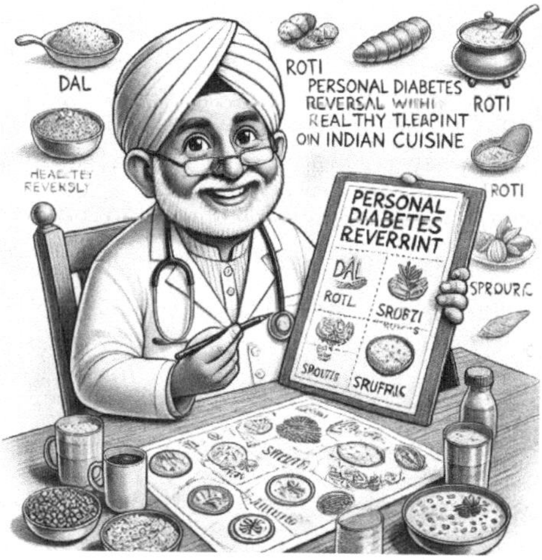

Ready for some kitchen magic? In this chapter, you will learn:

- Why mashed cauliflower > mashed potatoes
- The sneaky tricks to keeping your breakfast low-GI (hint: ditch the cereal)
- How to enjoy desserts without spiking your glucose (yes, it is possible—say hello to chocolate avocado mousse).

Pro Tip: Use apple cider vinegar before meals. It is like a glucose bodyguard—studies show it can reduce post-meal sugar levels.

When it comes to reversing diabetes, food is medicine. But the goal here is not to say goodbye to the foods you love—especially in a country as diverse as India, where each region celebrates its own culinary traditions. The idea is to adjust your meals by making smart substitutions, incorporating low-GI foods, and finding a balance between indulgence and health.

This chapter focuses on creating healthy, diabetes-friendly meals while still enjoying the flavors of North, South, East, and West India. Let us dive into Indian foods—those you should favor, those to limit, and practical swaps to keep your blood sugar levels stable without compromising on taste.

Understanding Carbs in Indian Cuisine

A typical Indian meal is carb-heavy, with rice, roti, and parathas taking center stage. But not all carbs are created equally simple carbs like white rice and refined flour (maida) cause quick glucose spikes, while complex carbs (whole grains and legumes) release sugar slowly, keeping your blood sugar levels stable.

Here is the plan: Swap high-GI foods for low-GI ones and make subtle changes that suit your local cuisine.

North India: Smart Choices for Diabetes Control

What's Popular

In North India, meals often revolve around parathas, rotis, rajma (kidney beans), chole (chickpeas), dals, and rich curries. Dairy products like paneer, ghee, and curd also feature prominently.

Smart Substitutions

- Swap parathas made with refined flour for multigrain rotis or bajra rotis (pearl millet). Bajra has a low GI and is high in fiber, which slows glucose absorption.
- Replace white rice with quinoa, brown rice, or steel-cut oats khichdi. These grains release glucose slowly.

- Choose curd (dahi) or Greek yogurt over sweetened lassi or packaged yogurt.
- Instead of aloo paratha, try stuffed methi or gobi paratha with less oil.
- Add plenty of fiber-rich vegetables (like spinach, cabbage, or bottle gourd) to dals and curries.

Sample Meal: Multigrain roti with rajma curry and a side of cucumber salad. Finish with a small bowl of unsweetened curd.

South India: Low-GI Twists for Classic Dishes

What's Popular

South India is known for idli, dosa, rice-based dishes, sambhar, rasam, and coconut-heavy gravies. Meals tend to be rich in carbohydrates, especially white rice.

Smart Substitutions

- Swap white rice for millet varieties (foxtail millet or little millet) in pongal and upma.
- Replace regular dosas with ragi dosa or adai (multi-lentil dosa)—both have a lower GI.
- Use whole red rice or brown rice instead of white rice for biryanis and idlis.
- Opt for vegetable-heavy sambhar and rasam to increase fiber and reduce the carb load.
- For snacks, replace murukku and vada with boiled chickpeas or sprout salads.

Sample Meal: A plate of ragi dosa with sambhar and a side of coconut chutney (in moderation).

East India: Managing Blood Sugar with Traditional Flavors

What's Popular

In the East, fish, rice, mustard gravies, and sweets like rasgulla and sandesh dominate the cuisine. Meals often include white rice and starchy vegetables like potatoes and yams.

Smart Substitutions

- Use brown rice or black rice (Chak-Hao) in place of polished white rice. Black rice is high in fiber and antioxidants.
- Swap sweetened desserts for fruit-based desserts with a sprinkle of cinnamon or a few unsweetened dates.
- Replace fried snacks with roasted muri (puffed rice) chaat loaded with cucumber, tomatoes, and sprouts.
- Add more non-starchy vegetables (like ridge gourd, pumpkin, and leafy greens) to your curries.
- Cook fish with less oil and bake or steam it instead of frying.

Sample Meal: Brown rice, steamed fish in mustard sauce, and stir-fried spinach side.

West India: Healthy Tweaks for Regional Delights

What's Popular

The cuisine in the West varies greatly, from theplas and dhoklas in Gujarat to vada pav and poha in Maharashtra. Coconut-based dishes are common in Goa.

Smart Substitutions

- Use whole-wheat theplas instead of regular ones, and pair them with unsweetened curd instead of sugary pickles.
- Replace poha with quinoa poha—quinoa has a lower GI and more fiber.
- Try dhokla made with besan (gram flour) or moong dal for a high-protein snack.
- Instead of vada pav, opt for vegetable cutlets made with sweet potatoes or chickpeas.
- Go for coconut milk-based curries in moderation, and balance them with plenty of vegetables.

Sample Meal: Moong dal dhokla with a side of mint chutney and a bowl of cucumber raita.

How to Build a Diabetes-Friendly Indian Plate

Use the Plate Method to build meals that are balanced and blood sugar friendly.

- ½ plate: Non-starchy vegetables (like greens, okra, or cabbage)
- ¼ plate: Protein (paneer, fish, eggs, or dals)
- ¼ plate: Healthy carbs (brown rice, millet roti, or quinoa)
- Add healthy fats: A spoon of ghee or some nuts.

This structure ensures your meals are rich in fiber, moderate in carbs, and packed with nutrients.

Snacking Smart: Healthy Indian Snack Ideas

When hunger strikes, avoid high-GI snacks like chips or sugary biscuits. Instead, try these:

- Roasted makhana (fox nuts) seasoned with spices.

- Sprouted moong salad with tomatoes and onions.
- A handful of almonds or walnuts
- Boiled chickpeas tossed with lemon and chaat masala.
- Buttermilk (chaas) or coconut water (in moderation)

Quick Breakfast Ideas for Busy Mornings

1. Vegetable oats upma with carrots, beans, and peas.
2. Besan chilla (gram flour pancake) with mint chutney.
3. Ragi porridge with unsweetened almond milk and berries.
4. A bowl of Greek yogurt with chia seeds and a few almonds.
5. Avocado toasted on whole grain bread with a sprinkle of chili flakes.

Diabetes-Friendly Desserts (Yes, You Can Indulge!)

It is okay to indulge occasionally if you choose wisely and watch portions. Here are a few options:

- Chia seed pudding with almond milk and a dash of cinnamon.
- Fruit salad with a sprinkle of roasted flax seeds.
- Baked apples with a spoon of Greek yogurt.
- Dark chocolate (70-85% cocoa)—one or two small squares.

Tips to Stay on Track with Indian Meals

1. Watch portion sizes: Stick to smaller servings of rice, rotis, and parathas.
2. Pair carbs with protein and fat: This reduces the glycemic load of your meal.
3. Increase fiber: Add more vegetables, seeds, and sprouts to your meals.

4. Cook with minimal oil: Use healthy oils like mustard, olive, or coconut oil in moderation.
5. Avoid late-night snacking: If you need a snack, opt for buttermilk or a handful of nuts.

Closing Thoughts: Enjoy Your Meals, Control Your Glucose

Eating healthily does not mean giving up on the foods you love. With a few smart tweaks, you can enjoy Indian cuisine without compromising your health. The goal is to balance your meals, focus on low-GI ingredients, and listen to your body's glucose responses through continuous monitoring. Over time, these changes will become habits—and you will find yourself enjoying your meals while keeping your blood sugar under control.

In the next chapter, we will explore exercise routines that complement your diet and help you stay on track with your diabetes reversal journey. Remember, the key is progress, not perfection. So, make minor changes, enjoy your food, and celebrate your wins—one meal at a time!

Chapter 7
The Exercise Equation – Moving to Manage Glucose and Protect Your Heart

Good news—you do not need a marathon to reverse diabetes. In fact, short bursts of exercise (HIIT or even dancing) are incredibly effective at burning glucose and improving insulin sensitivity.

And here is a tip: A brisk 15-minute walk after meals works like magic. It is easy, it is free, and you do not need a fancy gym membership.

Exercise is often touted as a magic pill for overall health—and with good reason. For people with diabetes, physical activity does more than just burn calories. It directly lowers blood glucose levels, improves insulin sensitivity, reduces body fat, and strengthens the heart. Exercise also plays a crucial role in reducing the risk of cardiovascular complications, which are common in people with diabetes. The right exercise plan can protect you against heart disease, high blood pressure, stroke, and even kidney problems.

This chapter will walk you through the best exercise strategies for diabetes reversal, with tailored advice for patients with heart disease, high blood pressure, or other complications. Let us lace up our shoes and get moving—because staying active is one of the most effective ways to outsmart glucose and protect your health.

Why Exercise is Essential for Diabetes Reversal

Physical activity lowers blood glucose in two ways:

1. Increase glucose uptake: Your muscles use glucose as fuel during exercise, pulling it from the bloodstream without needing much insulin.
2. Improves insulin sensitivity: Regular exercise makes your body more responsive to insulin, which means glucose enters your cells more efficiently.

In addition to these benefits, exercise:

- Reduces belly fat (a key contributor to insulin resistance).
- Improves heart health by reducing blood pressure and cholesterol.
- Lowers stress and improves mental well-being, which helps regulate blood sugar.
- Increases muscle mass, which burns more glucose even at rest.

How Much Exercise Do You Need?

The American Diabetes Association (ADA) recommends:

- 150 minutes of moderate-intensity aerobic exercise per week (about 30 minutes, 5 days a week).

- Strength training at least 2 days a week.
- Daily movement, even light activities like walking or stretching.

But do not worry if 150 minutes sounds overwhelming. Start small—even a 5-10 minute walk after meals can make a noticeable difference to your blood sugar levels.

Best Exercises for Diabetes Management and Heart Health

Let us break down the most effective exercises that lower blood sugar and protect your heart.

1. Aerobic Exercise: Improve Insulin Sensitivity and Heart Function

Aerobic exercises increase your heart rate and make you breathe faster. They improve cardiovascular health and help your muscles burn more glucose during and after your workout.

Examples of Aerobic Exercises

- Brisk walking: One of the simplest and most effective exercises for diabetes and heart health.
- Jogging or running: Ideal if your joints can manage it—boosts cardiovascular fitness.
- Cycling: Gentle on the knees and great for endurance.
- Swimming or water aerobics: Perfect for people with joint pain or arthritis.
- Dancing: A fun way to stay active without feeling like you are working out.

Pro Tip: Use a fitness tracker or CGM (Continuous Glucose Monitor) to track how your blood sugar responds to different aerobic activities.

How much?

- Start with 15-20 minutes of brisk walking after meals. Gradually increased to 30 minutes, 5 days a week.

2. Strength Training: Build Muscle, Burn Glucose, and Protect Your Heart

Building muscle is critical for people with diabetes. More muscle means your body burns more glucose even at rest. Strength training also improves bone health, balance, and insulin sensitivity.

Strength Training Exercises

- Bodyweight exercises: Squats, lunges, push-ups, and planks.
- Resistance bands: Great for beginners—light resistance with no need for heavy weights.
- Free weights or dumbbells: Start with small weights to build strength safely.
- Gym machines: If you have access to a gym, machines can help isolate specific muscle groups.

How much?

- Aim for 2-3 strength training sessions per week.
- Focus on all major muscle groups (legs, arms, back, chest, and core).

Tip for Heart Patients:
If you have heart disease, start with low-intensity strength exercises, and avoid holding your breath while lifting (this raises blood pressure).

3. Yoga and Stretching: Manage Stress and Improve Flexibility

Yoga offers both physical and mental benefits—it improves flexibility, reduces stress, and lowers blood pressure. For people with diabetes, yoga also helps regulate blood sugar by reducing cortisol levels (the stress hormone).

Recommended Yoga Poses for Diabetes and Heart Health

- Tadasana (Mountain Pose): Improves posture and balance.
- Bhujangasana (Cobra Pose): Stimulates digestion and blood circulation.
- Vrikshasana (Tree Pose): Builds balance and strengthens legs.
- Shavasana (Corpse Pose): Promotes relaxation and reduces stress.

How much?

- Practice 15-20 minutes of yoga 3-4 days a week.
- Add a 5-minute meditation session to lower cortisol levels and manage stress.

4. Walking: A Simple but Powerful Tool for Glucose Control

Walking after meals has been shown to reduce post-meal glucose spikes significantly. It is easy, accessible, and gentle on your joints, making it an excellent option for everyone, especially those with heart disease or high blood pressure.

How to Get Started:

- Post-meal walks: A 10-15 minute walk after meals can prevent glucose surges.
- Use interval walking (alternating between fast and slow walking) to boost cardiovascular fitness.

5. High-Intensity Interval Training (HIIT): Quick and Effective

If you are short on time, HIIT is a great option. It involves alternating short bursts of intense exercise with periods of rest. HIIT improves insulin sensitivity, helps with weight loss, and strengthens the heart.

Example HIIT Routine:

- 30 seconds of fast walking or jogging
- 30 seconds of slow walking (rest)
- Repeat for 10-15 minutes.

Caution for Heart Patients:

- If you have cardiovascular disease, consult your doctor before starting HIIT. Begin with moderate exercise and gradually increase intensity.

Managing Exercise with Other Health Conditions

Many people with diabetes also struggle with high blood pressure, heart disease, or joint problems. Here is how to stay active safely if you have additional health concerns:

1. Heart Disease:
    - Stick to moderate-intensity exercises (like walking, yoga, or swimming).
    - Avoid exercises that make you feel dizzy or short of breath.
    - Monitor your heart rate—stay in the target heart rate zone recommended by your doctor.
2. High Blood Pressure:
    - Avoid heavy weightlifting—opt for resistance bands instead.

   - Focus on aerobic activities like walking or swimming.
   - Do breathing exercises to lower my blood pressure.

3. Joint Pain or Arthritis:
   - Try low-impact exercises like swimming, cycling, or water aerobics.
   - Use resistance bands instead of weights to reduce joint strain.
   - Stretch regularly to improve mobility.

Exercise Timing: When is the Best Time to Work Out?

- Morning: Exercising on an empty stomach can improve insulin sensitivity. But if you have low glucose levels, eat a small snack first.
- After meals: A 15-minute walk after each meal prevents glucose spikes.
- Evening: Light activities in the evening can help improve sleep and glucose levels overnight.

Monitoring Glucose During Exercise

If you are using a CGM (Continuous Glucose Monitor), exercise is a wonderful way to see your glucose trends in action. Keep an eye on:

- Before exercise: If glucose is below 100 mg/dL, eat a small snack.
- During exercise: If you feel dizzy, fatigued, or shaky, stop and check your glucose.
- After exercise: Monitor how long your glucose stays low post-workout—this will help you fine-tune your routine.

Staying Motivated: Tips to Make Exercise a Habit

1. Find activities you enjoy: Dance, hike, swim, or play a sport—movement should be fun!
2. Set realistic goals: Start with small steps and build gradually.
3. Exercise with a friend: Working out with a friend keeps you accountable.
4. Track your progress: Use a fitness app or journal to log workouts and glucose changes.
5. Reward yourself: Celebrate small wins—whether it is a new workout outfit or a guilt-free smoothie.

The Bottom Line: Move More, Live Better

Exercise is a powerful tool in your diabetes reversal plan—and it comes with a host of benefits beyond blood sugar control. A healthy heart, improved mood, and better sleep are just a few of the rewards. Whether you prefer walking, strength training, yoga, or dance, the key is to move consistently and make it enjoyable.

Chapter 8
Mind over Muffin – Mental Health and Stress Control

Stress is like that annoying friend who crashes the party and spikes your blood sugar. Cortisol (the stress hormone) can make your body insulin resistant—even if you are eating perfectly. So, in this chapter, we will dive into:

- Mindful breathing exercises
- Why yoga is not just for Instagram.
- The magic of 8 hours of sleep (because no one makes healthy food choices when they are tired).

Managing diabetes is not just about diet, exercise, or glucose levels, it is also about managing your mind and emotions. Stress, anxiety, depression, and poor sleep are often part of the diabetes journey, and they play a much bigger role in blood sugar control than most people realize. Stress can raise cortisol levels, increase insulin resistance, and disrupt your glucose balance, making it harder to reverse diabetes.

This chapter will explore the powerful connection between mental health and diabetes, how stress impacts your glucose levels, and the practical strategies you can use to reduce stress, boost your mood, and sleep better. We will also discuss mindfulness practices, relaxation techniques, and how to manage emotional eating. Think of this chapter as your mental fitness plan—because a calm, focused mind is a key player in diabetes reversal.

The Stress-Glucose Connection: Why Stress Raises Blood Sugar

When stressed, your body triggers the "fight-or-flight" response. Your adrenal glands release cortisol (the stress hormone), which prepares your body to deal with a perceived threat by releasing more glucose into the bloodstream for quick energy.

But here is the problem:

- In modern life, stress often is not physical (like running from a tiger). It comes from work deadlines, financial issues, or family conflicts.
- That extra glucose is not burned so it stays in your bloodstream, raising your blood sugar levels.
- Chronic stress also makes your cells less responsive to insulin, contributing to insulin resistance.

The takeaway: Managing stress is not just about feeling good, it directly impacts your blood sugar. Learning to control your stress levels can improve insulin sensitivity and help you reverse diabetes.

The Vicious Cycle of Diabetes and Mental Health Issues

Living with diabetes can itself be stressful, leading to a cycle where stress and anxiety worsen blood sugar levels, and high glucose levels, in turn, worsen mood. Here is how the cycle works:

1. Diabetes burnout: Constantly managing medications, meals, and glucose levels can feel overwhelming.
2. Mood disorders: People with diabetes are more prone to anxiety and depression.
3. Emotional eating: Stress and anxiety can trigger cravings for high-carb comfort foods, spiking blood sugar.
4. Sleep disturbances: Poor glucose control can disrupt sleep, leading to fatigue and irritability the next day.
5. Increased glucose levels: The cycle continues as stress, poor sleep, and emotional eating raise blood sugar.

The good news? Breaking this cycle is possible with the right strategies—starting with stress management, mindfulness, and emotional resilience.

How to Manage Stress and Improve Mental Well-Being

Here are some evidence-based strategies for managing stress and improving mental health on your diabetes reversal journey.

1. Mindfulness and Meditation: Calm Your Mind, Lower Your Glucose

Mindfulness involves staying present in the moment without judgment. Studies show that mindfulness meditation lowers cortisol levels, improves insulin sensitivity, and helps people with diabetes make better food and lifestyle choices.

How to Get Started:

- Set aside 5-10 minutes daily to practice mindfulness.

- Focus on your breath—breathe slowly and deeply.
- Notice your thoughts without trying to change them. Simply observe.

Apps to Try:

- Headspace or Calm for guided meditation.
- My Life Meditation for quick, stress-relieving sessions.

2. Breathing Exercises: A Quick Way to Lower Stress

Breathing exercises can calm your nervous system and lower blood pressure and blood sugar.

Try This Simple Breathing Exercise:

1. Inhale deeply through your nose for 4 seconds.
2. Hold your breath for 4 seconds.
3. Exhale slowly through your mouth for 6-8 seconds.
4. Repeat this cycle for 5 minutes whenever you feel stressed.

Pro Tip: Pair this exercise with your glucose monitoring routine—check how your levels respond before and after deep breathing.

3. Yoga: A Holistic Approach to Stress and Blood Sugar Control

Yoga combines movement, breath control, and meditation to improve both mental and physical health. Research shows that practicing yoga can reduce blood glucose levels, lower blood pressure, and improve mood.

Recommended Yoga Poses for Stress Relief and Diabetes Control:

- Balasana (Child's Pose): Relieves stress and calms the mind.

- Setu Bandhasana (Bridge Pose): Lowers blood pressure and improves blood circulation.
- Shavasana (Corpse Pose): Promotes deep relaxation.
- Pranayama (breath control): Balances glucose levels through slow, mindful breathing.

Try practicing 15-20 minutes of yoga a few times a week to manage stress effectively.

4. Journaling: Get Your Thoughts on Paper

Journaling helps you process emotions, track triggers, and identify patterns in your stress and eating habits. It is a simple but powerful tool for mental clarity.

How to Use a Journal Effectively:

- Write down daily reflections—What made you feel stressed or happy today?
- Track emotional eating patterns—When do you crave sugary foods?
- Celebrate small wins—Record glucose improvements, workout sessions, or healthy meals.

5. Managing Emotional Eating: Outwit the Muffin Cravings

Emotional eating is when you eat to cope with feelings like boredom, sadness, or anxiety, rather than hunger. This can lead to glucose spikes and derail your diabetes reversal efforts.

How to Overcome Emotional Eating:

1. Identify triggers: Keep a journal of when emotional eating happens.
2. Find alternatives: When cravings strike, go for a walk, call a friend, or practice breathing exercises.

3. Keep healthy snacks on hand—like nuts, seeds, or yogurt—so you are not tempted by high-carb treats.
4. Be kind to yourself: Slip-ups happen. The goal is progress, not perfection.

6. Social Support: Do not Go It Alone

Having a dedicated support system makes it easier to stay on track with diabetes management. Share your journey with family, friends, or a support group. If you do not feel comfortable discussing your condition with friends, look for online communities where others are going through similar experiences.

7. Sleep: The Unsung Hero of Diabetes Control

Poor sleep can raise cortisol levels and reduce insulin sensitivity. Aim for 7-8 hours of quality sleep every night to keep your glucose levels stable.

Tips for Better Sleep:

- Stick to a consistent sleep schedule, even on weekends.
- Avoid screens (phones, tablets, TV) one hour before bed—blue light interferes with melatonin.
- Create a relaxing bedtime routine with light stretching or meditation.
- If you wake up during the night, avoid checking your phone—try deep breathing instead.

How CGM (Continuous Glucose Monitoring) Can Help with Stress Management

A CGM device can help you track how stress impacts your glucose levels in real time. For example:

- If you notice a glucose spike after an argument or a stressful meeting, use breathing exercises to bring it down.
- Over time, you will become more aware of how specific situations or emotions affect your glucose, allowing you to respond proactively.

Managing Depression and Anxiety: When to Seek Help

If you are experiencing persistent sadness, anxiety, or loss of interest in activities you once enjoyed, it is important to seek professional help. Diabetes and mental health are linked and addressing both is essential for your well-being. Talk to your doctor about therapy, counseling, or medications if needed.

The Role of Laughter: A Natural Blood Sugar Booster

Here is some great news: Laughter lowers blood sugar! Research shows that laughter improves blood flow, reduces cortisol, and boosts mood. Watch a comedy show, laugh with friends, or share a funny meme—your glucose monitor might just thank you.

Key Takeaways: Manage Your Mind, Manage Your Diabetes

- Stress management is crucial for reversing diabetes—it lowers cortisol, improves insulin sensitivity, and helps regulate glucose levels.
- Mindfulness, meditation, yoga, and journaling are powerful tools to reduce stress and improve emotional well-being.
- Healthy sleep habits support blood sugar control and reduce cravings.
- Social support and professional help are essential, do not hesitate to reach out if you need it.
- And remember: Laughter is free medicine, use it often!

In the next chapter, we will dive into intermittent fasting, time-restricted eating, and how to trick your body into healing naturally. Stay calm, stay mindful—and keep outwitting that muffin! 😊

Chapter 9
Time-Restricted Eating & Fasting – Trick Your Body into Healing

Here is the secret: When you stop eating for a while, your body burns through its sugar reserves and starts improving insulin sensitivity. This chapter will cover:

- How to ease into intermittent fasting (without feeling like a zombie)
- The best fasting windows for glucose control
- Tips to survive cravings—because yes, they will come, and yes, you can outsmart them.

For centuries, humans have thrived by alternating between feasting and fasting. Today, however, we live in a world where food is available 24/7—and this constant access to calories contributes to blood sugar spikes, insulin resistance, and weight gain. But here is the exciting news: you can use fasting strategically to heal your body, improve insulin sensitivity, and reverse diabetes. This chapter will walk you through the science, benefits, and practical methods of fasting—with a focus on making it easy, sustainable, and safe.

The Science of Fasting: Why It Works for Diabetes

Fasting is not about starvation—it is about giving your body a break from constantly processing food. During periods without food, your blood sugar levels stabilize, and insulin levels drop, allowing your body to access stored fat for energy. This process, called lipolysis, helps reverse insulin resistance and improves glucose metabolism.

Here is what happens during the fasting:

1. Blood sugar drops, reducing the need for insulin.
2. Stored glycogen (sugar in the liver) gets used up.
3. Your body switches to burning fat for energy.
4. Insulin sensitivity improves, making your cells more efficient at using glucose.

In addition to these metabolic benefits, fasting helps lower inflammation, improve heart health, and supports weight loss, all of which contributes to reversing diabetes.

Types of Fasting: Choose What Works for You

Not all fasting methods are the same. Here are some popular fasting strategies, along with their pros and cons.

1. Time-Restricted Eating (TRE)

With TRE, you eat all your meals within a set 8-12 hour window each day. For example, you might eat between 9 AM and 7 PM and fast the remaining hours. This allows your body to rest and repair overnight.

Benefits:

- Easy to integrate into daily life.
- Reduces late-night snacking, which spikes glucose levels.
- Improves insulin sensitivity and promotes weight loss.

How to Start:

- Begin with a 12-hour window (e.g., 8 AM to 8 PM) and gradually narrow it to 8-10 hours if comfortable.
- Drink water, herbal tea, or black coffee during fasting hours to stay hydrated.

2. 16:8 Intermittent Fasting

In this method, you fast for 16 hours and eat within an 8-hour window—for example, 11 AM to 7 PM. Many people skip breakfast and start their day with lunch.

Benefits:

- Increases fat-burning and promotes weight loss.
- It prevents glucose spikes from eating frequently.
- Simple to follow, just skip one meal a day.

How to Start:

- Gradually extend your fasting window—start at 14:10 (14 hours fasting, 10 hours eating) before moving to 16:8.
- Monitoring how your glucose responds—CGM (Continuous Glucose Monitoring) can be especially helpful here.

3. 5:2 Fasting

In 5:2 fasting, you eat normally for 5 days a week and restrict calories to 500-600 on two non-consecutive days.

Benefits:

- Allows flexibility—eat normally most of the week.
- Encourages fat loss and improves glucose control.

How to Start:

- On fasting days, eat small, nutrient-dense meals like vegetable soups, salads, or smoothies.
- Make sure to stay hydrated and monitor glucose levels to avoid drops.

4. Alternate-Day Fasting (ADF)

In ADF, you alternate between a normal eating day and a fasting day (where you consume 500-600 calories).

Benefits:

- Promotes rapid fat loss and improves insulin sensitivity.
- May reverse diabetes faster, though it can be challenging to follow.

How to Start:

- Begin with one fasting day a week, then gradually increase.
- Ensure fasting days include high-protein, fiber-rich foods to maintain energy.

Fasting Safely with Diabetes: What You Need to Know

Fasting can be highly effective for reversing diabetes, but it must be done carefully—especially if you are taking medications. Here are some important safety tips:

1. Consult Your Doctor: If you are on medications (like insulin or metformin), your doctor may need to adjust your doses to avoid hypoglycemia (low blood sugar).
2. Monitor Your Glucose Levels: Use your CGM or glucometer regularly during fasting to track how your body is responding.
3. Stay Hydrated: Dehydration can increase blood sugar—drink plenty of water during fasting periods.
4. Watch for Symptoms: If you feel dizzy, weak, or extremely hungry, break your fast with a small, balanced meal.

Fasting for People with Heart Disease or Hypertension

If you have heart disease or high blood pressure, fasting can still be beneficial, but you need to be cautious:

1. Stick to light fasting methods like Time-Restricted Eating (TRE) or 16:8 fasting.
2. Avoid long fasting periods without medical supervision—your blood pressure medications may need to be adjusted.
3. Focus on heart-healthy foods while eating windows, such as leafy greens, nuts, seeds, and olive oil.
4. Avoid salty foods that could raise blood pressure—especially after breaking fast.

What to Eat When You Break Your Fast

It is important to break your fast with balanced meals to avoid glucose spikes. Here are some healthy, diabetes-friendly meal ideas for breaking your fast:

1. Vegetable and Lentil Soup: High in fiber and keeps glucose levels stable.
2. Avocado Toast on Whole Grain Bread: Healthy fats reduce glucose absorption.

3. Chickpea or Quinoa Salad: Rich in protein and fiber.
4. Greek Yogurt with Berries: Low-GI option with a good balance of protein and carbs.
5. Stir-Fried Vegetables with Tofu or Paneer: Light, nutritious, and blood sugar friendly.

How Fasting Affects Your Metabolism

Fasting has a positive effect on your metabolism. It helps:

- Reduce insulin levels, allowing your body to burn fat more effectively.
- Trigger autophagy (a cellular cleaning process), which removes damaged cells and reduces inflammation.
- Improve lipid profiles—lowering cholesterol and triglycerides, which benefits heart health.

However, if you fast too often or restrict calories too severely, it can slow your metabolism. That is why it is essential to find a balance that works for your lifestyle.

Managing Cravings and Hunger During Fasting

Hunger is natural during fasting, especially in the beginning. Here are some tips to manage cravings:

1. Drink water—often thirst feels like hunger.
2. Add a pinch of salt to your water if you feel lightheaded (this helps replenish electrolytes).
3. Distract yourself with activities like reading, walking, or meditation.
4. Eat high-protein, high-fiber meals during your eating window to keep hunger at bay.
5. Drink herbal teas or black coffee (in moderation) to suppress appetite.

Key Takeaways: Make Fasting Work for You

- Start slowly gradually increase your fasting window as your body adapts.
- Use CGM to monitor your glucose and fine-tune your fasting routine.
- Always break your fast with healthy, balanced meals to avoid glucose spikes.
- If you have heart disease or hypertension, consult your doctor before trying extended fasts.
- Remember: Fasting is not about deprivation—it is about giving your body time to heal.

Final Thoughts: Fasting as a Tool, not a Rule.

Fasting is a powerful tool for reversing diabetes and improving overall health, but it is not a rigid rule. The goal is to find a fasting method that fits your lifestyle, whether that is skipping breakfast, eating within an 8-hour window, or fasting a few days a week. As you experiment with fasting, listen to your body and adjust your plan accordingly. Over time, fasting will become a natural part of your routine—and your lifestyle.

Chapter 10
The Role of Medications – When You Need a Boost

Note: We are against self-medication of any type, especially it needs to be re-emphasized that this chapter is for information only and not for self-treatment

Medications are great sidekicks, but the goal is to reduce or eliminate the need for them. We will discuss:

- When medications make sense
- How to taper off meds safely
- Why collaborating with your doctor is non-negotiable (No DIY medication experiments, please!).

While diet, exercise, fasting, and stress management are powerful tools for reversing diabetes, medications still play a critical role in managing blood sugar levels, especially in the initial stages of your journey. The goal is to reduce or eliminate your dependence on medications, but for some individuals, medications may be essential in preventing complications like heart disease, kidney problems, or nerve damage while lifestyle changes take effect.

In this chapter, we will discuss the diverse types of diabetes medications, when and how they should be used, how to taper off medications safely, and what to do if you are living with comorbidities like hypertension, high cholesterol, or heart disease.

Why Medications are Often Necessary (At Least Temporarily)

Even if you are committed to reversing diabetes through lifestyle changes, medications can serve as a bridge. They control blood sugar in the short term, preventing serious complications while you work on improving insulin sensitivity through diet, fasting, and exercise.

Medications may be essential if:

- Your A1C levels are exceedingly high (above 8%).
- You experience frequent glucose spikes that put you at risk of complications.
- You have other conditions like hypertension or cardiovascular disease.
- You need to delay while you make sustainable lifestyle changes.

The idea is to use medications as part of a comprehensive plan—not a long-term crutch.

Types of Diabetes Medications and How They Work

Here is a breakdown of the most common medications used in diabetes management, with a focus on how they can complement your lifestyle efforts.

1. Metformin: The First Line of Defense

Metformin is often the first medication prescribed to people with Type 2 diabetes. It works by:

- Decreasing glucose production in the liver.
- Improving insulin sensitivity so your cells absorb glucose more effectively.
- Reducing post-meal glucose spikes.

Why It is Helpful:

- Metformin is safe, inexpensive, and effective.
- It does not cause weight gain or hypoglycemia (low blood sugar).

When to Use:

- It is often prescribed when A1C is above 6.5%.
- If your lifestyle changes are working, your doctor may reduce the dose or discontinue it.

2. Sulfonylureas: Stimulating Insulin Production

Sulfonylureas (like glipizide and glimepiride) stimulate your pancreas to release more insulin.

Pros:

- They help lower blood sugar quickly.
- Useful if your pancreas is still capable of producing insulin.

Cons:

- They can cause hypoglycemia (low blood sugar).
- Long-term use can lead to weight gain and further beta-cell exhaustion.

When to Use:

- Sulfonylureas are often prescribed short-term while you transition to lifestyle changes.
- Close glucose monitoring is essential to prevent hypoglycemia.

3. GLP-1 Receptor Agonists: Weight Loss and Glucose Control

Medications like semaglutide (Ozempic) and liraglutide (Victoza) mimic the GLP-1 hormone, which regulates blood sugar and appetite.

Benefits:

- Reduces glucose spikes after meals.
- Suppresses appetite and promotes weight loss.
- May reduce the risk of cardiovascular events.

When to Use:

- These medications are useful if you are struggling with obesity or heart disease.
- GLP-1 agonists can complement fasting or time-restricted eating by controlling hunger.

4. SGLT2 Inhibitors: Protect Your Heart and Kidneys

SGLT2 inhibitors (like dapagliflozin and canagliflozin) help your kidneys excrete excess glucose through urine.

Benefits:

- Lowers blood sugar without causing hypoglycemia.
- Reduces blood pressure and promotes weight loss.
- Protects against heart failure and kidney disease.

When to Use:

- Recommended for people with diabetes and cardiovascular disease or chronic kidney disease.

5. Insulin: Managing Severe Cases or Beta-Cell Failure

While insulin is typically associated with Type 1 diabetes, it may also be prescribed for people with severe Type 2 diabetes. Insulin injections help:

- Lower blood sugar when other medications are insufficient.
- Prevent complications from uncontrolled glucose levels.

Challenges:

- Weight gain is a common side effect.
- Risk of hypoglycemia with improper dosing.

When to Use:

- Insulin is usually a last resort if your beta cells are exhausted or if your glucose levels remain dangerously high despite other interventions.

Managing Medications with Comorbidities: A Holistic Approach

Many people with diabetes also have other conditions like hypertension, high cholesterol, or heart disease. Here is how to manage these conditions alongside diabetes.

1. Diabetes and Hypertension

High blood pressure (hypertension) is common in people with diabetes, increasing the risk of heart disease and stroke. Medications like ACE inhibitors and ARBs can help lower blood pressure and protect your kidneys.

Tips:

- Exercise and weight loss can reduce both blood pressure and blood sugar levels.
- Lower your salt intake to prevent hypertension.

2. Diabetes and Heart Disease

If you have cardiovascular disease (CVD), some diabetes medications like SGLT2 inhibitors and GLP-1 agonists offer additional heart protection.

Tips:

- Focus on a heart-healthy diet with lots of fruits, vegetables, whole grains, and healthy fats.
- Monitor cholesterol levels and take statins if prescribed.
- Avoid intense exercise without your doctor's approval, start with moderate activities like walking or yoga.

3. Diabetes and Kidney Disease

High blood sugar can damage the kidneys, leading to diabetic nephropathy. If you have signs of kidney disease, your doctor may adjust your diabetes medications to prevent further damage.

Tips:

- SGLT2 inhibitors can protect kidney function.
- Monitoring your protein intake—too much can strain your kidneys.

- Stay hydrated to support kidney health.

How to Safely Taper Off Medications

As you make progress with diet, exercise, and fasting, your doctor may decide to reduce or stop your medications. Here is how to do it safely:

1. Collaborate closely with your doctor: Never stop medications on your own—sudden changes can cause dangerous glucose spikes.
2. Track your glucose levels: Use CGM or regular glucose monitoring to assess how your body responds to medication changes.
3. Adjust gradually: Taper off medications slowly to allow your body to adapt.
4. Celebrate small wins: Each reduction in medication is a step closer to your goal of reversing diabetes.

Recognizing the Signs of Hypoglycemia (Low Blood Sugar)

As you reduce medications, it is essential to watch for signs of hypoglycemia, especially if you are using insulin or sulfonylureas.

Symptoms of Hypoglycemia:

- Dizziness or lightheadedness
- Sweating or shaking
- Confusion or irritability
- Rapid heartbeat
- Blurred vision

What to Do:

- Check your glucose levels immediately.
- Eat a quick-acting carb like glucose tablets, fruit juice, or candy.
- Recheck the glucose after 15 minutes—if it is still low, eat more carbs.

When Medications are No Longer Needed

Many people successfully reduce or eliminate their medications as they reverse their diabetes. If your A1C remains below 5.7% for several months and you are maintaining a healthy lifestyle, your doctor may declare you "in remission." At this point, your focus will shift to preventing relapses by sticking to your healthy habits.

Key Takeaways: Using Medications Wisely

- Medications are an important part of diabetes management, but they should complement—not replace—lifestyle changes.
- Your goal is to reduce or eliminate medications over time by improving your insulin sensitivity and stabilizing glucose levels.
- Monitor your progress closely with CGM and regular check-ups.
- Collaborate with your doctor to adjust medications safely, especially if you have other conditions like heart disease or hypertension.
- Celebrate every step forward—even small reductions in medication are wins on your reversal journey!

In the next chapter, we will explore real-life success stories of people who have reversed their diabetes and the lessons you can learn from their journeys. You have come this far—keep going and remember that every choice you make today brings you closer to a diabetes-free life.

Chapter 11
Success Stories
Diabetes Reversals

What We Can Learn from Them

Inspiration alert! Meet people who have brought their A1C levels back to normal—through diet, exercise, and determination. From former fast-food addicts to dessert lovers, these stories prove that diabetes does not stand a chance when you take control.

There is nothing more motivating than hearing from people who have walked the same path and successfully reversed their Type 2 diabetes. Each journey is different, but they all share common elements—commitment, small but consistent changes, and a willingness to try new strategies. In this chapter, we will meet real people who reversed diabetes through lifestyle changes. You will also learn the lessons from their experiences, the challenges they faced, and how they overcame setbacks.

The life like stories are to encourage self-care and remind you that reversal is not only possible, it's achievable. Let us dive into these inspiring journeys and extract the key strategies that worked for them.

Success Story #1: Rajesh from Mumbai – Reversing Diabetes with 16:8 Fasting and Walking

Initial Condition:

- Age: forty-five
- A1C: 8.2%
- Weight: 85 kg (187 lbs)
- Medications: Metformin and glimepiride

The Journey: Rajesh, a software engineer from Mumbai, was diagnosed with diabetes after a routine health check-up. His busy work life meant long hours at the desk, stress, and late-night snacking. Initially, he felt overwhelmed but decided to give intermittent fasting (16:8) and post-meal walking a try.

- He skipped breakfast and ate his first meal at 11 AM, finishing his last meal by 7 PM.
- After lunch and dinner, he made it a habit to walk for 20 minutes around his apartment building.
- He reduced his intake of rice and bread, swapping them for quinoa and millet-based rotis.

Results:

- In 6 months, Rajesh's A1C dropped from 8.2% to 5.8%.
- He lost 10 kg (22 lbs) and discontinued his glimepiride medication under his doctor's supervision.
- Today, Rajesh continues his 16:8 routine and enjoys weekend hikes with his family

Key Takeaways:

- Intermittent fasting can improve insulin sensitivity and control glucose spikes.
- Daily movement, even light walking, makes a substantial difference.
- It is possible to manage diabetes while working full-time if you create simple, sustainable habits.

Success Story #2: Priya from Bengaluru – From Carb Cravings to Smart Substitutions

Initial Condition:

- Age: thirty-eight
- A1C: 7.6%
- Struggled with emotional eating and carb cravings.
- Medications: Metformin

The Journey: Priya had a history of emotional eating—she reached for sweets and fried snacks whenever she felt stressed. She wanted to reverse her diabetes but knew she had to address her cravings. Here is what she did:

- She replaced her evening snacks with roasted makhana (fox nuts) and nuts like almonds and walnuts.
- For sweets, she switched to dark chocolate (85% cocoa) and made fruit-based desserts like chia seed pudding.
- She started practicing yoga three times a week to reduce stress and improve her emotional well-being.

Results:

- Priya's A1C dropped from 7.6% to 6.1% within 4 months.
- Her cravings were reduced, and she felt more in control of her food choices.

- She now uses mindful eating practices to prevent emotional eating.

Key Takeaways:

- Smart food substitutions can satisfy cravings without raising blood sugar.
- Managing stress through yoga or mindfulness improves both glucose control and emotional health.
- Consistency is more important than perfection—slight changes add up.

Success Story #3: Anil from Delhi – Rebuilding His Health with Strength Training and Diet

Initial Condition:

- Age: fifty-two
- A1C: 9.0%
- Weight: 95 kg (209 lbs)
- Medications: Insulin and metformin

The Journey: Anil was frustrated with his insulin dependence and wanted to reduce his medication. His doctor recommended strength training to build muscle and improve insulin sensitivity. Anil hired a trainer who introduced him to bodyweight exercises and dumbbell workouts.

- He started with light exercises like squats and push-ups and gradually increased his intensity.
- He cut down on sugary drinks and replaced them with buttermilk and herbal teas.
- He followed the Plate Method—filling half his plate with vegetables, a quarter with lean protein, and a quarter with healthy carbs like quinoa.

Results:

- In 8 months, Anil lost 15 kg (33 lbs) and lowered his A1C from 9.0% to 6.2%.
- He reduced his insulin dosage by 50% and is now working towards eliminating it completely.
- Anil feels stronger, more energetic, and motivated to stay active.

Key Takeaways:

- Strength training builds muscle, which improves glucose control and burns more calories at rest.
- Balanced meals prevent glucose spikes—use the Plate Method for portion control.
- Gradual progress works, do not work for perfection, just keep moving forward.

Success Story #4: Amina from Kolkata – Managing Diabetes with Time-Restricted Eating and Heart-Healthy Foods

Initial Condition:

- Age: forty-eight
- A1C: 8.5%
- High blood pressure and cholesterol
- Medications: Metformin, statins, and antihypertensives

The Journey: Amina was diagnosed with diabetes along with hypertension and high cholesterol, putting her at risk for cardiovascular disease. She adopted Time-Restricted Eating (TRE) and focused on heart-healthy foods.

- She ate between 10 AM and 6 PM and avoided late-night snacking.

- Amina incorporated walnuts, flaxseeds, and olive oil into her meals for heart health.
- She practiced morning breathing exercises to manage her blood pressure.

Results:

- After 6 months, Amina's A1C dropped from 8.5% to 6.0%.
- Her blood pressure stabilized, and her doctor reduced her statin dosage.
- Amina now walks every morning and enjoys cooking healthy meals with her family.

Key Takeaways:

- Time-Restricted Eating helps lower glucose levels and manage cravings.
- Heart-healthy fats (like nuts, seeds, and olive oil) are essential for people with diabetes and heart disease.
- Mind-body practices (like breathing exercises) benefit both blood pressure and glucose control.

Lessons Learned: What Do These Success Stories Teach Us?

1. Start Small and Build Gradually:
   - Big changes can feel overwhelming. Focus on one habit at a time, like walking after meals or skipping sugary drinks.
2. Consistency Matters More Than Perfection:
   - Setbacks are normal—what matters is getting back on track without guilt.
3. Exercise is Powerful Medicine:

    - Even light exercises like walking, yoga, or bodyweight workouts improve insulin sensitivity and glucose control.

4. Track Your Progress:
    - Use a CGM or glucometer to understand how your body responds to different foods and activities.
5. Manage Stress and Sleep:
    - Good mental health is crucial—stress reduction techniques and quality sleep are essential for diabetes reversal.
6. Collaborate Closely with Your Doctor:
    - As your glucose levels improve, medications may need to be adjusted. Never stop medications without consulting your doctor.

Your Story Could Be Next!

Each of these success stories shows that reversing diabetes is possible—with commitment, patience, and the right strategies. No two journeys are the same, but the principles are universal: move more, eat smarter, manage stress, and stay consistent.

You do not have to be perfect. All you need to do is take small, sustainable steps every day. Your journey might have ups and downs, but with persistence, you will get there. And who knows? One day, you might inspire others with your own success story.

In the next chapter, we will provide a 30-Day Reversal Plan with detailed meal ideas, workout routines, and mindset tips to help you kickstart your diabetes-free life. You are there, let us finish strong!

Chapter 12
Your 30-Day Reversal Plan – Recipes, Workouts, and Mindful Moments

It is time to get practical. This chapter includes:

- Daily meal plans
- Easy workout routines
- CCG-friendly meal prep tips
- Weekly check-ins to monitor progress.

We have provided the reversal plan, please follow it under your physician's guidance.

Welcome to the 30-Day Diabetes Reversal Plan, your roadmap to getting your blood sugar under control and starting your journey toward long-term remission. This plan is not about crash diets or extreme routines, it is about building sustainable habits that become part of your lifestyle.

In the next 30 days, you will focus on low-GI meals, gentle but consistent exercise, stress reduction, and tracking progress. Whether you are just starting or looking to solidify your progress, this plan will help you take actionable steps every day.

How the 30-Day Plan Works

Every day includes:

- Balanced meals focused on low-GI foods.
- Daily movement, with easy exercises you can do at home or outdoors.
- Mindful practices to manage stress.
- Tracking your progress with a journal or glucose monitor.

The plan is divided into four weekly phases, each with a specific focus to gradually build your new lifestyle. Let us dive into the daily routines, meal ideas, exercise strategies, and mindfulness tips that will guide you.

Phase 1 (Days 1-7): Kickstart Your Routine

Focus: Establish meal timing and basic movement habits.

- Daily Goal: Start Time-Restricted Eating (TRE)—eat within a 10-hour window (e.g., 9 AM to 7 PM).
- Exercise: 15-minute walk after meals.
- Mindfulness: Practice 5 minutes of deep breathing each morning.

Sample Daily Routine – Day 1

- Breakfast (9:00 AM):
  Ragi dosa with coconut chutney and a boiled egg.

- Lunch (1:00 PM):
  Quinoa salad with grilled chicken, cucumber, tomatoes, and olive oil dressing.
- Snack (4:00 PM):
  Handful of almonds and green tea.
- Dinner (6:30 PM):
  Brown rice with dal, sautéed spinach, and cucumber raita.
- Post-Dinner:
  15-minute walk + 5 minutes of stretching.

Phase 2 (Days 8-14): Add Strength and Balance

Focus: Build strength and introduce more balanced meals.

- Daily Goal: Add a 20 minute strength workout (twicc a week).
- TRE Adjustment: Narrow your eating window to 8 hours (e.g., 10 AM to 6 PM).
- Mindfulness: Start gratitude journaling—write down three things you are grateful for each day.

Strength Workout – Day 9

- Bodyweight squats: two sets of ten
- Push-ups (modified if needed): two sets of 8.
- Plank hold: thirty seconds.
- Lunges: two sets of ten per leg

Meal Plan – Day 10

- Breakfast: Oats porridge with chia seeds and fresh berries.
- Lunch: Paneer tikka with vegetable stir-fry.
- Snack: Buttermilk (chaas) with roasted makhana.

- Dinner: Fish curry with black rice and steamed broccoli.

Phase 3 (Days 15-21): Focus on Stress and Sleep

Focus: Optimize sleep and stress management.

- Daily Goal: Aim for 7-8 hours of quality sleep each night.
- Exercise: Add evening yoga sessions for relaxation.
- Mindfulness: Practice guided meditation before bed.

Evening Yoga Routine – Day 16

- Child's Pose (Balasana): 1 minute
- Seated Forward Bend (Paschimottanasana): one minute.
- Legs Up the Wall (Viparita Karani): 2 minutes
- Shavasana (Corpse Pose): three minutes.

Tip: Use a sleep tracker or CGM to monitor how improved sleep affects your blood sugar levels.

Phase 4 (Days 22-30): Fine-Tune and Maintain

Focus: Refine your routines and prepare for long-term success.

- Daily Goal: Experiment with intermittent fasting (16:8) if it feels comfortable.
- Exercise: Incorporate interval walking or light jogging.
- Mindfulness: Reflect on the month—what worked, and what did not?

Day 25 – Example Meal and Activity Plan

- Breakfast (11:00 AM): Greek yogurt with walnuts and a drizzle of honey.
- Lunch (2:00 PM): Lentil and vegetable soup with a whole-wheat thepla.

- Snack (4:30 PM): A small piece of 85% dark chocolate and green tea.
- Dinner (6:00 PM): Baked sweet potatoes with sautéed mushrooms and a side salad.
- Evening: Interval walking—1 minute brisk, 2 minutes slow, repeated for 15 minutes.

Weekly Check-ins: Track Your Progress

Every week, take 10-15 minutes to reflect on your progress. Use the following questions to guide your check-in:

1. How did my glucose levels respond this week?
2. Did I stick to my meal plan and exercise routine?
3. What challenges did I face, and how did I manage them?
4. What is one thing I can improve next week?

Grocery List for the 30-Day Plan

Here is a handy list of staples you will need for the month:

- Whole grains: Quinoa, millet, brown rice, oats
- Legumes: Lentils, chickpeas, kidney beans
- Vegetables: Spinach, broccoli, cauliflower, zucchini, tomatoes, cucumbers
- Fruits: Berries, apples, pears, pomegranates
- Proteins: Eggs, chicken, fish, paneer, tofu
- Healthy fats: Avocado, olive oil, ghee, nuts, seeds
- Beverages: Green tea, herbal tea, buttermilk

Tips for Success

1. Plan Your Meals in Advance: Batch-cook meals on weekends to save time during busy weekdays.

2. Stay Flexible: If you miss a workout or indulge occasionally, do not stress—just get back on track the next day.
3. Listen to Your Body: Adjust your eating window or exercise routine as needed to suit your energy levels.
4. Use CGM Data: Track how your blood sugar responds to different foods and activities will help you fine-tune your plan.
5. Celebrate Small Wins: Each healthy choice is progress. Acknowledge your efforts along the way.

What to Expect After 30 Days

By the end of this 30-day plan, you can expect:

- Improved glucose control—fewer spikes and more stable readings.
- Weight loss (if needed) and reduced belly fat.
- Better energy levels throughout the day.
- Reduced stress and better sleep.
- Lower A1C levels—you may need less medication or none (consult your doctor).

Your New Beginning: A Lifestyle, not a Diet

The 30-Day Reversal Plan is not the end of the journey, it is the beginning of a new lifestyle. These habits will set the foundation for long-term health and diabetes remission. The key to success is consistency, not perfection. Some days will be harder than others, and that is okay. If you stay committed to progress, you will continue to see results.

In the next chapter, we will discuss how to maintain these habits for life and what to do when things get off track. Congratulations on making it through the plan—your future self will thank you!

Chapter 13
Maintenance Mode – Staying Diabetes - Free for Life

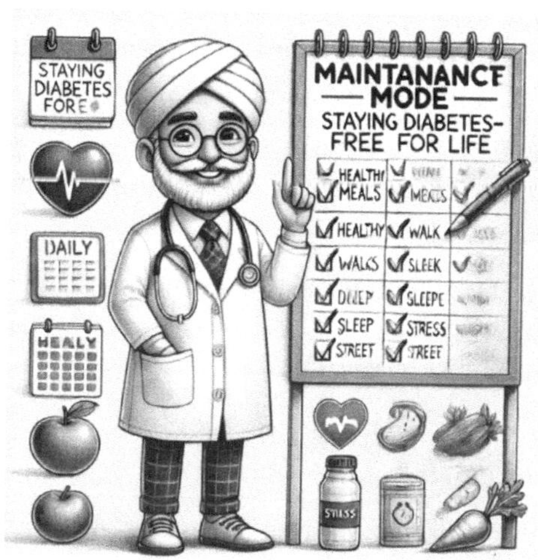

You have done it! Now let us make sure you stay diabetes-free. This chapter covers:

- How to manage occasional indulgences without guilt
- The importance of regular glucose monitoring (even when you feel great)
- Staying motivated for the long haul (hint: make it fun!).

Congratulations! You have made it through the 30-Day Reversal Plan and taken significant steps to manage or reverse your diabetes. But here is the truth: reversing diabetes is not the finish line—it is a new beginning. The challenge now is to maintain your progress and prevent relapses by turning the habits you have built into a sustainable lifestyle.

This chapter is your maintenance guide. We will cover how to stay consistent, what to do when life throws you off track, how to indulge occasionally without guilt, and ongoing health check-ups to ensure you stay diabetes-free for life. Think of this phase as health maintenance mode—where the goal is not just remission, but vibrant, sustainable well-being.

Why Maintenance Matters: The Risk of Relapse

Studies show that lifestyle changes can reverse diabetes in many cases. However, if old habits creep back in, blood sugar levels can rise again, leading to a relapse. Maintenance mode helps you avoid reverting to old patterns by reinforcing what worked during your reversal journey.

Your goal is to:

- Keep A1C levels below 5.7%.
- Maintain consistent glucose control (below 140 mg/dL post-meals).
- Continue building strength, reducing stress, and improving sleep.

How to Maintain Your Progress: Key Strategies

1. Stick to the Fundamentals: Diet, Exercise, and Stress Control

Maintaining remission means continuing the same lifestyle habits that brought you success.

Diet: Eat for Long-Term Health

- Follow the 80/20 rule: Eat healthy 80% of the time, allowing for small indulgences occasionally.
- Stick to low-GI foods—these are your best friends.

- Plan balanced meals using the Plate Method—half vegetables, one-quarter protein, one-quarter complex carbs.
- Keep sugary and processed foods as rare treats to avoid triggering glucose spikes.

Exercise: Keep Moving Consistently

- Aim for 150 minutes of aerobic exercise per week (like walking, swimming, or cycling).
- Continue strength training twice a week to maintain muscle mass and insulin sensitivity.
- If life gets busy, remember that short bursts of activity (like 10-minute walks after meals) still count.

Stress Control: Stay Mindful

- Stick with yoga, meditation, or breathing exercises to manage stress.
- Use journaling to reflect on your progress and challenges.
- Spending time with friends, family, or in nature—social connections are essential for mental well-being.

2. Plan for Life's Curveballs

Life is unpredictable—travel, holidays, family events, or stressful periods can disrupt your routine. The key is to have a plan for these situations.

How to Manage Social Events or Travel

- Choose healthier options when dining out—opt for grilled dishes, salads, and skip sugary drinks.
- Carry healthy snacks like nuts, seeds, or fruit to avoid temptation.

- Walk after meals to manage glucose, even if it is just around the hotel lobby.

What to Do After a Setback

- Do not panic if you indulge or miss a few workouts. A single meal or week off-track will not undo your progress.
- Check your glucose levels to assess the impact, then get back to your routine the next day.
- Learn from the experience—what triggered the slip, and how can you prepare differently next time?

3. Monitor Your Health Regularly

Monitoring is essential to maintain remission and catch any warning signs early. Keep an eye on your blood sugar, weight, and other health markers to stay on track.

Ongoing Health Check-Ups

- A1C test every 3-6 months to ensure levels remain below 5.7%.
- Blood pressure and cholesterol checks at least once a year, especially if you have a history of cardiovascular issues.
- Annual eye and kidney exams to detect any early signs of complications.

Using CGM (Continuous Glucose Monitoring)

- Check your glucose after meals occasionally to ensure it stays within range.
- Use CGM to identify new triggers—like stress, sleep disturbances, or new foods—and adjust accordingly.

4. Celebrate Wins, Big and Small

A critical part of maintaining your progress is to celebrate milestones along the way. This keeps you motivated and reinforces positive behavior.

How to Celebrate Without Food Rewards

- Treat yourself to non-food rewards—like a new workout outfit, a spa day, or a weekend trip.
- Reflect on your achievements regularly—journal about the improvements in your health, energy, and mood.
- Share your success with friends or in online communities to inspire others on their journey.

5. Indulge Mindfully—Without Guilt

Indulgence is part of life, and occasional treats won't derail your progress. The key is to enjoy them mindfully.

How to Indulge Smartly

- Choose low-GI desserts (like dark chocolate or chia seed pudding) to minimize glucose spikes.
- Watch portion sizes—a small piece of cake is fine but avoid going overboard.
- Time your indulgences wisely—enjoy treats after a meal with protein or fiber to slow glucose absorption.

Pro Tip: If you know you will be indulging, plan a short workout or walk afterward to burn off excess glucose.

6. Stay Connected to Your "Why"

Your "why" is your North Star—the reason you started your diabetes reversal journey in the first place. Whether it is to have more energy, avoid medications, or enjoy life with your loved ones, keep this motivation in mind as you continue.

Tips to Stay Connected to Your "Why"

- Visualize your goals, imagine the future version of yourself, living diabetes-free.
- Create reminders, keep a photo, quote, or journal entry that reflects your progress.
- Talk about your goals with friends or family, they will encourage you to stay on track.

7. Know When to Adjust Your Plan

Life changes—whether it is aging, work demands, or family responsibilities. What worked in the past may need adjustment over time. Be open to modifying your routine as needed.

When to Adjust Your Plan:

- If your glucose levels start rising, revisit your eating habits or increase physical activity.
- If you hit a plateau, try new workouts (like yoga, swimming, or interval walking) to keep things interesting.
- If stress levels increase, double down on mindfulness practices and social support.

8. Work with Your Healthcare Team

Your healthcare team remains an essential part of your journey, even in remission. They will help you monitor your progress and provide guidance if new challenges arise.

When to Consult Your Doctor:

- If your glucose levels increase unexpectedly.
- If you are struggling with stress, sleep, or emotional eating.

- To adjust medications or supplements as needed.

What to Expect in the Long Run

Here is what long-term success looks like:

- Consistently normal A1C and fasting glucose levels.
- Reduced or eliminated need for medications.
- Steady energy levels and improved mental well-being.
- A sustainable lifestyle that includes healthy eating, regular exercise, and stress management.

The key is to stay curious and adaptable. Your health will evolve, and so will your needs. Listen to your body, track your progress, and adjust as needed.

Final Words: A New Chapter, A New You

Congratulations, you have not only reversed your diabetes but also transformed your life. This is not just about managing a condition; it is about living fully, joyfully, and healthily.

Remember: You have the tools, knowledge, and experience to stay in remission. There may be bumps along the way, but with consistency, self-compassion, and the right mindset, you will continue to thrive.

Your journey is not over, it is just the beginning. You now have the freedom to enjoy life without the burden of diabetes holding you back. Celebrate every small victory, stay connected to your goals, and keep moving forward—because the best is yet to come!

Chapter 14
You are Not Alone – The Power of Coaching and Support on Your Journey

Preamble: Why Coaching Makes All the Difference

You have come this far, and that is incredible. But let us be honest, the journey to health is not always easy. Some days will feel tough. There will be moments when you question your progress, feel tempted to go back to old habits, or simply need a push in the right direction. That is where coaching comes in.

The truth is, even the best of us needs support, accountability, and motivation. Just like athletes rely on coaches to guide them to success, your health journey can be supercharged with the right kind of coaching. It is not about being perfect, it is about having someone by your side to remind you why you started, celebrate your wins, and help you overcome setbacks.

The Importance of Coaching: A Helping Hand When You Need It Most

Health coaching offers more than just advice, it is about personal support, accountability, and guidance. Coaching helps you stay focused, develop new habits, and adjust your strategies when life gets in the way.

Here's how coaching makes a difference:

1. Accountability: Knowing someone is tracking your progress encourages you to stay committed.
2. Motivation: A coach provides positive reinforcement and reminds you of your goals on tough days.
3. Personalized Advice: Your journey is unique—tailored coaching ensures the strategies align with your needs.
4. Emotional Support: Coaches help you overcome mental roadblocks, from stress eating to negative thinking.
5. Sustainable Change: Coaching focuses on long-term success, helping you build habits that last a lifetime.

Coaching as a Group: Strength in Numbers

If you are navigating diabetes alongside family or friends, coaching together can be a game-changer. Having a support network of people who understand your struggles makes the journey easier and more enjoyable. When you share the experience with loved ones, it fosters accountability and encouragement.

Benefits of Group Coaching with Family and Friends:

- Shared goals create stronger motivation.
- You will learn from each other's successes and challenges.

- Cooking and exercising together makes the process fun and sustainable.
- It strengthens relationships as you work toward a shared purpose.
- It is easier to build healthy family habits that benefit everyone, not just those with diabetes.

Tip: Even if your family members do not have diabetes, their support will make a significant difference. Group coaching helps everyone adopt healthier lifestyles—and prevents future diabetes risks for your loved ones.

Call to Action: Let Us Do This Together

This is your moment to take the next step. You have already come so far—do not let doubt or hesitation stop you from achieving your goals. If you feel you need a little extra push, personalized coaching or group coaching with family and friends can supercharge your success.

I want you to know: You are not alone. I am here to help you stay on track, celebrate your progress, and find solutions when life gets challenging. Whether it is a one-on-one coaching session or group coaching for your entire family, the goal is to guide you toward the healthy, vibrant life you deserve.

Why Coaching Matters: Even the Strongest Need Support

Even the most motivated individuals need help from time to time. Think of athletes, entrepreneurs, or anyone striving for greatness, they all have coaches who push them forward, even when they feel stuck. Your journey is no different. There is no shame in asking for help, it is a sign of strength.

Coaching is about:

- Reminding you of your progress when you lose sight of how far you have come.
- Helping you refocus when life gets overwhelming.
- Encouraging you to keep going, even when you hit roadblocks.

It is okay to feel like you need extra support. That is what coaching is for—to keep you motivated and move forward, no matter what.

How to Get Started with Coaching

Ready to take action? Here is how we can work together:

1. One-on-One Coaching: Personalized guidance and strategies based on your specific needs, lifestyle, and challenges.
2. Group Coaching: Gather your family, friends, or community members to create a shared journey toward health.
3. Accountability Check-Ins: Regular follow-ups to track progress, troubleshoot challenges, and celebrating wins.
4. Customized Meal and Activity Plans: Practical, tailored recommendations to fit your routine.
5. Ongoing Motivation: I will be there to cheer you on, even when you feel stuck.

Coaching with a Purpose: Making It Fun and Sustainable

This journey is not about strict diets or punishing workouts, it is about finding what works for you and making it enjoyable. Together, we will create a plan that fits your life and keeps you engaged and inspired. We will make sure that every milestone—no matter how small—gets celebrated.

And do not forget: This is not just about you. It is about empowering your family and community to adopt healthier habits, creating a ripple effect of positive change.

Final Thoughts: You Deserve This Support

You have already shown your strength by committing yourself to this journey. Now, it is time to take the next step and embrace the power of coaching. Whether it is through individual coaching or group sessions, I am here to guide, support, and cheer you on.

This is your moment. You do not have to do it alone, and you do not have to figure everything out by yourself. Together, we will make sure you stay on the path to a diabetes-free life.

Your Call to Action: Let Us Get Started Today

If you are ready to move forward and take control of your health, now is the time. Do not wait for the perfect moment, the perfect moment is now. Reach out today, and let us start building the healthier, happier version of yours.

Remember: Coaching is not about fixing you, it is about unlocking your potential and helping you become the best version of yourself. You have the power to achieve your goals—and I am here to help you every step of the way.

Let us do this together. Your future self will thank you.

For getting coaching email to drsibia@gmail.com.

Chapter 15
Reversal or Remission

Note on the Use of "Diabetes Reversal"

In this book, we use the term "diabetes reversal" to convey a powerful message of hope and empowerment. While the term "remission" is technically more accurate from a medical standpoint, we believe "reversal" better captures the transformative potential of lifestyle changes for people with type 2 diabetes.

Here is why:

- Psychological Impact: "Reversal" suggests a more complete and permanent change than "remission," which can imply a temporary state. This positive framing can inspire readers to take ownership of their health and commit to long-term lifestyle changes.

- Motivational Power: "Reversal" emphasizes the possibility of regaining control over one's health. It suggests that diabetes is not a life sentence, but a condition that can be significantly improved or even overcome through dedicated effort.
- Accessibility: "Reversal" is a more straightforward and easily understood term for the public. It avoids medical jargon and resonates with a wider audience.

Important Clarification:

While we use "reversal" throughout the book, we acknowledge that achieving lasting remission requires ongoing commitment to healthy habits. Type 2 diabetes is a complex condition, and ongoing monitoring and adjustments may be necessary to maintain healthy blood sugar levels.

Our aim is to inspire and empower readers to take control of their health and achieve the best possible outcomes. We believe that the term "diabetes reversal," used responsibly and with appropriate context, serves this purpose effectively.

Chapter 16
What More Do You Want?

In my over 40 years of practice I came across, guided, coached and helped many diabetic, blood pressure, heart disease, Gut health, Cognitive Decline, Anxiety, Depression, Osteoporosis, Back/Joint Pain, Osteoarthritis, Sleep, Low Energy, Chronic Fatigue, Stress, Brain Fog, Headaches, smoking, post covid, patients, successfully to eliminate or reduce their medication with alert efforts and live a healthy life. I am not ashamed to share that I learnt many tips from my learned patients. The insights helped me understand dos and don'ts for diabetics. For success honesty and sincere effort are essential to bear fruit.

I hope you enjoyed reading "Reversing Diabetes: A Journey Back to Health". If you did, I would love to hear your feedback. What do you like most about the book? What would you like to see added in future editions?

I am also interested in hearing from you about your own experiences with diabetes. What challenges have you faced? What strategies have you used to manage your diabetes?

I would be happy to include your suggestions in future editions of this book. You can send your feedback to me at drsibia@gmail.com.

I would also like to invite you to contribute a chapter to a future edition of this book - If you had a unique perspective on diabetes, I would love to hear from you. Your chapter could be about anything related to diabetes, from your firsthand experiences to the latest research findings.

I believe that by sharing our experiences and knowledge, we can help more people live healthy lives. I hope you will join me in this effort.

Thank you for reading!

Dr. Sukhbindar Singh Sibia, MBBS, MD

President: International ECP Association

Director: Sibia Medical Centre

Email: info@sibiamedicalcentre.com

Web: www. sibiamedicalcentre.com

www.cytotrontreatment.com

Video Library: www.youtube.com/sibiamedicalcentre/

Annexures 1

Vegetarian Foods and Their Glycemic Index

Low GI (â‰¤55)	Moderate GI (56-69)	High GI (â‰¥70)
Broccoli (GI 15)	Sweet Corn (GI 60)	Potatoes (GI 85)
Carrots (GI 35)	Banana (GI 62)	Pumpkin (GI 75)
Chickpeas (GI 28)	Pineapple (GI 66)	Watermelon (GI 76)
Lentils (GI 29)	Brown Rice (GI 68)	Parsnips (GI 97)
Tomatoes (GI 15)	Beetroot (GI 64)	Instant Rice (GI 85)
Spinach (GI 15)	Green Peas (GI 54)	Rutabaga (GI 72)
Cabbage (GI 10)	Bulgur (GI 55)	Rice Cakes (GI 82)
Mushrooms (GI 10)	Oatmeal (GI 58)	White Bread (GI 75)
Soybeans (GI 16)	Sweet Potato (GI 63)	White Rice (GI 73)
Peanuts (GI 14)	Papaya (GI 59)	Cornflakes (GI 81)
Zucchini (GI 15)	Mango (GI 60)	Crispy Rice Cereal (GI 82)
Celery (GI 15)	Parsnips (GI 58)	French Fries (GI 75)
Cauliflower (GI 15)	Whole Wheat Bread (GI 69)	Mashed Potatoes (GI 83)
Eggplant (GI 15)	Barley (GI 55)	Rice Pasta (GI 78)
Onions (GI 10)	Couscous (GI 65)	Polenta (GI 72)

Green Beans (GI 30)	Grapes (GI 59)	Millet Porridge (GI 70)
Bell Peppers (GI 10)	Figs (GI 61)	Puffed Wheat (GI 80)
Asparagus (GI 15)	Kiwi (GI 58)	Pretzels (GI 83)
Snow Peas (GI 22)	Plantains (GI 66)	Macaroni (GI 78)
Plums (GI 24)	Cantaloupe (GI 65)	Scones (GI 92)
Oranges (GI 40)	Honeydew Melon (GI 62)	Bagels (GI 72)
Apples (GI 36)	Turnips (GI 55)	Tapioca (GI 70)
Pears (GI 38)	Amaranth (GI 57)	Crispbread (GI 74)
Grapefruit (GI 25)	Quinoa (GI 53)	Pineapple Juice (GI 78)
Peaches (GI 28)	Sorghum (GI 58)	Ripe Bananas (GI 72)
Berries (GI 40)	Millet (GI 57)	Rice Noodles (GI 72)
Apricots (GI 30)	Butternut Squash (GI 63)	Tapioca Pudding (GI 85)
Cherries (GI 22)	Pumpkin Seeds (GI 60)	Crackers (GI 70)
Kidney Beans (GI 24)	Sunflower Seeds (GI 59)	Coconut Water (GI 71)
Black Beans (GI 30)	Cashews (GI 56)	Baked Potatoes (GI 85)

Annexures 2

Fruits and Their Glycemic Index

Low GI (â‰¤55)	Moderate GI (56-69)	High GI (â‰¥70)
Apples (GI 36)	Mango (GI 60)	Watermelon (GI 76)
Pears (GI 38)	Banana (GI 62)	Ripe Pineapple (GI 72)
Cherries (GI 22)	Pineapple (GI 66)	Overripe Banana (GI 75)
Grapefruit (GI 25)	Ripe Banana (GI 62)	Dates (GI 73)
Oranges (GI 40)	Figs (GI 61)	Papaya Juice (GI 72)
Plums (GI 24)	Plantains (GI 66)	Jackfruit (GI 75)
Peaches (GI 28)	Honeydew Melon (GI 62)	Tamarind (GI 70)
Berries (GI 40)	Cantaloupe Melon (GI 65)	Durian (GI 75)
Strawberries (GI 41)	Raisins (GI 64)	Mango Juice (GI 73)
Blackberries (GI 25)	Dates (GI 62)	Fruit Cocktail (GI 72)
Apricots (GI 30)	Lychee (GI 57)	Pawpaw (GI 78)
Kiwi (GI 50)	Guava (GI 59)	Ripe Plantains (GI 70)
Grapes (GI 53)	Nectarines (GI 58)	Canned Pineapple (GI 75)
Prunes (GI 29)	Tangerines (GI 57)	Canned Peaches (GI 79)
Cranberries (GI 47)	Pineapple Juice (GI 66)	Pineapple Slices (GI 78)

Cantaloupe (GI 50)	Melon (GI 65)	Persimmon (GI 74)
Papaya (GI 42)	Starfruit (GI 59)	Overripe Melon (GI 70)
Blueberries (GI 53)	Passionfruit (GI 56)	Canned Pears (GI 71)
Pomegranate (GI 53)	Mulberries (GI 58)	Canned Apricots (GI 74)
Lemons (GI 20)	Dragon Fruit (GI 60)	Juiced Grapes (GI 74)

Annexure 3

Non-Vegetarian Foods and Their Glycemic Index

Low GI (â‰¤55)	Moderate GI (56-69)	High GI (â‰¥70)
Eggs (GI 0)	Turkey Sausage (GI 56)	Fried Fish (GI 70)
Chicken Breast (GI 0)	Chicken Nuggets (GI 58)	Processed Chicken Sausages (GI 74)
Turkey (GI 0)	Breaded Fish Fillet (GI 62)	Breaded Shrimp (GI 75)
Salmon (GI 0)	Crab Cakes (GI 59)	Canned Crab with Sauce (GI 76)
Tuna (GI 0)	Lamb Sausage (GI 57)	Fried Calamari (GI 72)
Shrimp (GI 0)	Fish Sticks (GI 60)	Tempura Fish (GI 80)
Beef (GI 0)	Canned Tuna in Oil (GI 57)	Fish Patty (GI 78)
Pork (GI 0)	Smoked Salmon (GI 55)	Fast Food Burger Patty (GI 73)
Lamb (GI 0)	Duck Sausage (GI 60)	Chicken Fries (GI 76)
Duck (GI 0)	Fish Fingers (GI 63)	Canned Tuna with Sauce (GI 72)
Sardines (GI 0)	Tilapia Nuggets (GI 61)	Battered Fish (GI 82)
Mackerel (GI 0)	Processed Crab Cakes (GI 59)	Tempura Shrimp (GI 85)
Cod (GI 0)	Shrimp Fritters (GI 58)	Popcorn Shrimp (GI 84)
Lobster (GI 0)	Canned Salmon (GI 57)	Chicken Patties (GI 75)

Crab (GI 0)	Fried Oysters (GI 60)	Chicken Strips (GI 74)
Octopus (GI 0)	Fish Cakes (GI 62)	Pre-cooked Fish Fillet (GI 80)
Scallops (GI 0)	Chicken Tenders (GI 64)	Spicy Fish Bites (GI 83)
Clams (GI 0)	Salmon Patty (GI 56)	Ready-to-eat Shrimp Bites (GI 78)
Oysters (GI 0)	Turkey Patty (GI 60)	Fried Chicken Wings (GI 81)
Quail (GI 0)	Lamb Chops Breaded (GI 59)	Breaded Calamari (GI 82)
Anchovies (GI 0)	Catfish Bites (GI 61)	Frozen Fish Sticks (GI 79)
Venison (GI 0)	Breaded Squid Rings (GI 63)	Breaded Haddock (GI 74)
Goose (GI 0)	Canned Sardines in Oil (GI 58)	Salmon Nuggets (GI 77)
Rabbit (GI 0)	Turkey Meatballs (GI 65)	Deep Fried Tuna Balls (GI 80)
Trout (GI 0)	Grilled Shrimp Skewers (GI 58)	Instant Fried Chicken (GI 73)

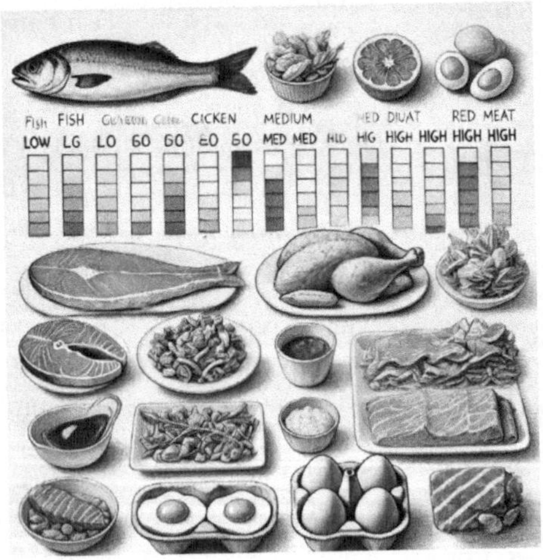

Annexure 4

Nutrition Values of Vegetarian Foods

Food Item	Calories (kcal)	Protein (g)	Carbohydrates (g)	Fat (g)	Fiber (g)
Broccoli (100g)	34	2.8	6.6	0.4	2.6
Carrots (100g)	41	0.9	9.6	0.2	2.8
Spinach (100g)	23	2.9	3.6	0.4	2.2
Sweet Potato (100g)	86	1.6	20.1	0.1	3
Chickpeas (100g)	164	8.9	27.4	2.6	7.6
Lentils (100g)	116	9	20.1	0.4	7.9
Tofu (100g)	76	8	1.9	4.8	0.3
Quinoa (100g)	120	4.4	21.3	1.9	2.8
Almonds (100g)	576	21.2	21.6	49.4	12.5
Walnuts (100g)	654	15	13.7	65.2	6.7
Oats (100g)	389	16.9	66.3	6.9	10.6
Brown Rice (100g)	111	2.6	23	0.9	1.8
Peas (100g)	81	5.4	14.5	0.4	5.7

Mushrooms (100g)	22	3.1	3.3	0.3	1
Avocado (100g)	160	2	8.5	14.7	6.7
Pumpkin (100g)	26	1	6.5	0.1	0.5
Cabbage (100g)	25	1.3	5.8	0.1	2.5
Tomato (100g)	18	0.9	3.9	0.2	1.2
Cucumber (100g)	16	0.7	3.6	0.1	0.5
Bell Pepper (100g)	31	1	6	0.3	2.1
Zucchini (100g)	17	1.2	3.1	0.1	1.1
Green Beans (100g)	31	1.8	7	0.2	3.4
Cauliflower (100g)	25	1.9	5	0.3	2.3
Eggplant (100g)	24	1	5.9	0.2	2.5
Beetroot (100g)	43	1.6	9.6	0.2	2.8
Artichokes (100g)	47	3.3	10.5	0.2	5.4
Brussels Sprouts (100g)	43	3.8	8.4	0.3	3.7
Okra (100g)	33	2	7.5	0.2	3.2
Asparagus (100g)	20	2.2	3.9	0.1	2.1

Celery (100g)	14	0.7	3	0.1	1.6
Kale (100g)	49	4.3	10	0.4	4.3
Parsley (100g)	36	3.1	6	0.7	3.6
Radish (100g)	16	1	4	0.1	1.2
Turnip (100g)	28	1.5	14	0.3	1.8
Leeks (100g)	45	5	10.1	0.1	8
Seaweed (100g)	121	11	8.5	5	5
Edamame (100g)	486	16.5	42.1	30	34.4
Chia Seeds (100g)	534	18.3	28.9	42.2	27.3
Flax Seeds (100g)	573	17	26	49.7	11.8

Annexures 5

Nutrition Values of Fruits

Fruit Item	Calories (kcal)	Protein (g)	Carbohydrates (g)	Fat (g)	Fiber (g)
Apple (100g)	52	0.3	13.8	0.2	2.4
Banana (100g)	89	1.1	22.8	0.3	2.6
Orange (100g)	47	0.9	11.8	0.1	2.4
Strawberries (100g)	32	0.7	7.7	0.3	2
Blueberries (100g)	57	0.7	14.5	0.3	2.4
Grapes (100g)	69	0.6	18.1	0.2	0.9
Pineapple (100g)	50	0.5	13.1	0.1	1.4
Mango (100g)	60	0.8	15	0.4	1.6
Watermelon (100g)	30	0.6	7.6	0.2	0.4
Peach (100g)	39	0.9	9.5	0.3	1.5
Plum (100g)	46	0.7	11.4	0.2	1.4
Kiwi (100g)	61	1.1	14.7	0.5	3
Cherries (100g)	50	1	12.2	0.3	1.6
Papaya (100g)	43	0.5	10.8	0.1	1.7

Avocado (100g)	160	2	8.5	14.7	6.7
Raspberries (100g)	52	1.2	11.9	0.6	6.5
Blackberries (100g)	43	1.4	9.6	0.4	5.3
Pomegranate (100g)	83	1.7	18.7	1.2	4
Cantaloupe (100g)	34	0.8	8.2	0.2	0.9
Guava (100g)	68	2.6	14.3	0.9	5.4

Annexures 6

Nutrition Values of Nuts

Nut Item	Calories (kcal)	Protein (g)	Carbohydrates (g)	Fat (g)	Fiber (g)
Almonds (100g)	576	21.2	21.6	49.4	12.5
Walnuts (100g)	654	15	13.7	65.2	6.7
Cashews (100g)	553	18.2	30.2	43.9	3.3
Pistachios (100g)	562	20	27.2	45.4	10.3
Hazelnuts (100g)	628	15	16.7	60.8	9.7
Macadamia Nuts (100g)	718	7.9	13.8	75.8	8.6
Brazil Nuts (100g)	656	14.3	12.3	66.4	7.5
Pecans (100g)	691	9.2	13.9	72	9.6
Pine Nuts (100g)	673	13.7	13.1	68.4	3.7
Chestnuts (100g)	213	2.4	45.5	2.2	8.1

Annexures 7

Nutrition Values of Eggs

Egg Item	Calories (kcal)	Protein (g)	Carbohydrates (g)	Fat (g)	Fiber (g)
Chicken Egg (whole, 100g)	143	12.6	0.7	9.5	0
Chicken Egg (white, 100g)	52	10.9	0.7	0.2	0
Chicken Egg (yolk, 100g)	322	15.9	3.6	26.5	0
Duck Egg (whole, 100g)	185	13.6	1.4	13.8	0
Quail Egg (whole, 100g)	158	13	0.4	11.1	0
Turkey Egg (whole, 100g)	171	13.4	1.2	11.9	0
Ostrich Egg (whole, 100g)	155	12.2	0.7	10.9	0

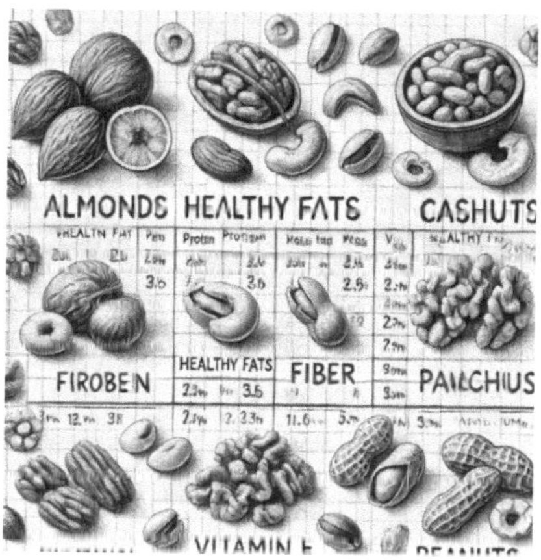

Annexures 8

Nutrition Values of Fish and Non-Vegetarian Foods

Food Item	Calories (kcal)	Protein (g)	Carbohydrates (g)	Fat (g)	Fiber (g)
Salmon (100g)	208	20.4	0	13	0
Tuna (100g)	132	29	0	0.9	0
Cod (100g)	82	18.1	0	0.7	0
Mackerel (100g)	205	19	0	13.9	0
Sardines (100g)	208	25	0	11.5	0
Chicken Breast (100g)	165	31	0	3.6	0
Turkey (100g)	135	28	0	3	0
Duck (100g)	337	19	0	28.4	0
Beef (100g)	250	26	0	20	0
Lamb (100g)	294	25	0	23	0
Pork (100g)	242	27	0	14	0
Shrimp (100g)	99	24	0	0.3	0
Crab (100g)	87	18	0	0.8	0
Lobster (100g)	77	16	0	0.6	0
Scallops (100g)	69	12	0	0.5	0
Quail (100g)	134	20	0	5	0
Goat (100g)	143	27	0	3	0

Pigeon (100g)	142	21	0	4	0
Rabbit (100g)	119	22	0	3.5	0
Goose (100g)	161	23	0	6	0
Venison (100g)	158	26	0	2	0
Octopus (100g)	82	14.9	0	1	0
Clams (100g)	74	12.8	5.1	1	0
Oysters (100g)	68	8.9	4.2	2	0
Cuttlefish (100g)	79	16	1	1.5	0

Annexures 9

Nutrition Values of Dairy Items

Dairy Item	Calories (kcal)	Protei n (g)	Carbohyd rates (g)	Fat (g)	Fibe r (g)
Whole Milk (100g)	61	3.2	4.8	3.3	0
Skim Milk (100g)	34	3.4	5	0.1	0
Cheddar Cheese (100g)	402	25	1.3	33	0
Mozzarella Cheese (100g)	280	28	2.2	17	0
Butter (100g)	717	0.9	0.1	81	0
Yogurt (Plain, 100g)	59	3.5	3.6	0.4	0
Greek Yogurt (100g)	97	10	3.6	5	0
Cream (Heavy, 100g)	340	2.8	2.8	37	0
Cottage Cheese (100g)	98	11	3.4	4.3	0
Ice Cream (Vanilla, 100g)	207	3.5	24	11	0

Annexures 10

Nutrition Values of Beverages

Beverage Item	Calories (kcal)	Protein (g)	Carbohydrates (g)	Fat (g)	Fiber (g)
Black Coffee (100g)	2	0.1	0	0	0
Green Tea (100g)	1	0	0.2	0	0
Orange Juice (100g)	45	0.7	10.4	0.1	0.2
Apple Juice (100g)	46	0.1	11	0.1	0.1
Coca-Cola (100g)	42	0	10.6	0	0
Milkshake (Chocolate, 100g)	116	3.4	19	3.8	0.4
Beer (100g)	43	0.5	3.6	0	0
Wine (Red, 100g)	85	0.1	2.6	0	0
Energy Drink (100g)	52	0.4	13	0.1	0
Smoothie (Mixed Fruit, 100g)	60	0.7	13.5	0.2	1.2

Annexures 11

Nutrition Values of Exotic Beverages

Beverage Item	Calories (kcal)	Protein (g)	Carbohydrates (g)	Fat (g)	Fiber (g)
Kombucha (100g)	16	0.2	3	0.1	0.1
Coconut Water (100g)	19	0.7	3.7	0.2	1.1
Matcha Latte (100g)	74	3.2	9.4	2.5	0.8
Chai Tea (100g)	60	1	13.2	2.1	1.5
Tamarind Juice (100g)	46	0.4	11.8	0.1	0.7
Aloe Vera Juice (100g)	15	0.1	3.5	0.1	0.4
Hibiscus Tea (100g)	2	0.4	0.5	0.1	0.3
Baobab Juice (100g)	44	0.6	9.8	0.3	0.6
Acai Smoothie (100g)	70	1.5	15	1.8	2
Yerba Mate (100g)	10	0.2	2	0.1	0.2

Annexure 12

Types of diabetes:

1. Type 1 Diabetes

- **Cause**: Type 1 diabetes is an autoimmune condition in which the immune system attacks and destroys insulin-producing beta cells in the pancreas.
- **Characteristics**: The body cannot produce insulin, leading to high blood glucose levels.
- **Onset**: Typically diagnosed in children and young adults but can occur at any age.
- **Management**: Requires lifelong insulin therapy, along with blood sugar monitoring, diet, and exercise.

2. Type 2 Diabetes

- **Cause**: Type 2 diabetes results from insulin resistance, where the body's cells do not respond effectively to insulin. Over time, insulin production decreases.
- **Characteristics**: The body can produce insulin, but it is either insufficient or not used effectively.
- **Onset**: Usually occurs in adults over 45, but now increased cases are seen in younger people due to lifestyle factors.
- **Management**: Managed through lifestyle changes (diet, exercise), oral medications, and sometimes insulin therapy.

3. Gestational Diabetes

- **Cause**: Hormonal changes during pregnancy make cells more resistant to insulin.
- **Characteristics**: Develops during pregnancy and usually resolves after childbirth but increases the risk of type 2 diabetes later.
- **Onset**: Occurs during the second or third trimester of pregnancy.
- **Management**: Managed through dietary changes, physical activity, and sometimes insulin or oral medications.

4. LADA (Latent Autoimmune Diabetes in Adults)

- **Cause**: Like type 1 diabetes, LADA is an autoimmune condition where the immune system attacks insulin-producing cells, but it progresses more slowly.
- **Characteristics**: Sometimes called type 1.5 diabetes, as it shares features of both type 1 and type 2 diabetes.
- **Onset**: Typically diagnosed in adults over thirty.
- **Management**: Initially managed with lifestyle changes and oral medications, but insulin therapy is usually needed as it progresses.

5. MODY (Maturity-Onset Diabetes of the Young)

- **Cause**: MODY is caused by a genetic mutation affecting insulin production, inherited in an autosomal dominant manner.
- **Characteristics**: It resembles type 2 diabetes but occurs at a younger age and is not related to obesity.
- **Onset**: Usually diagnosed in adolescents and young adults under twenty-five.

- **Management**: Often managed with oral medications, lifestyle changes, and sometimes insulin therapy depending on the specific type of MODY.

6. Secondary Diabetes

- **Cause**: Secondary diabetes results from other medical conditions or medications that affect insulin production or glucose regulation.
- **Examples**:
    - **Pancreatic Diseases**: Conditions like pancreatitis, pancreatic cancer, or cystic fibrosis.
    - **Endocrine Disorders**: Conditions like Cushing's syndrome and acromegaly.
    - **Medications**: Prolonged use of corticosteroids, antipsychotic drugs, and some cancer treatments.
- **Management**: Treatment focuses on the underlying cause along with standard diabetes management methods.

7. Prediabetes

- **Cause**: Prediabetes occurs when blood sugar levels are higher than normal but not high enough for a diabetes diagnosis.
- **Characteristics**: Prediabetes indicates an increased risk of developing type 2 diabetes, as well as heart disease and stroke.
- **Onset**: Can occur in both adults and children, often linked to lifestyle factors.
- **Management**: Often reversible through lifestyle changes, such as weight management, diet, and physical activity.

8. Neonatal Diabetes

- **Cause**: Neonatal diabetes is a rare form caused by genetic mutations affecting insulin production in newborns.
- **Characteristics**: Different from type 1 diabetes, it typically occurs within the first six months of life and can be either transient or permanent.
- **Onset**: Diagnosed in infants.
- **Management**: Managed with insulin or other specific medications depending on the type of genetic mutation.

Summary

Each type of diabetes has unique causes, onset, and management requirements. While type 1 and type 2 are the most common, other types like gestational diabetes, LADA, and MODY highlight the diverse nature of the condition. Understanding the type of diabetes is essential for tailored treatment and effective management.

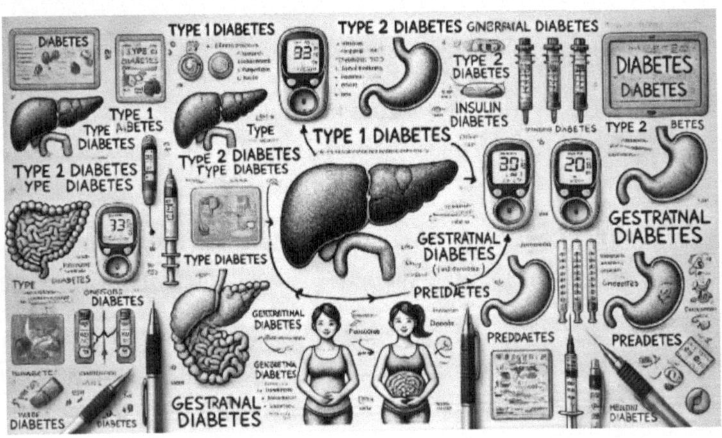

Annexure 13

Countries with the highest rate of diabetes

- China — over one billion
- India — over one billion
- U.S. — 338 million
- Indonesia — 275 million
- Pakistan — 235 million

Country with the lowest rate of diabetes

African region currently has the lowest prevalence of diabetes at 4.5%.

Prevalence of Diabetes in India's population (according to a 2023 Lancet study)

- Diabetes - 11.4% of the population
- Prediabetes - 15.3% of the population

States with the highest prevalence of diabetes:

Goa - 26.4%

Puducherry (26.3%)

Kerala (25.5%)

Diabetes by location: More common in urban areas than in rural areas.

Diabetes by education: Prevalence is lower among the poorer and less educated, as compared to those from the socially backward groups.

Diabetes and awareness and treatment:

- Among those with diabetes, 27.5% are aware.
- 21.5% are taking treatment.
- Seven percent have their diabetes under control.

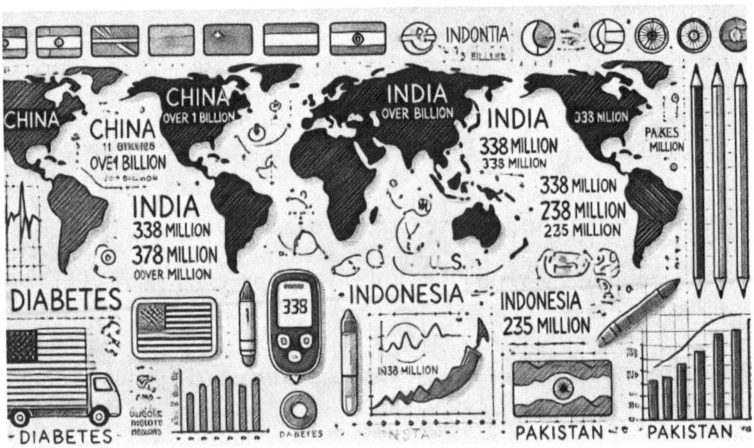

Annexure 14

Causes of Diabetes

Diabetes is a complex condition caused by a combination of genetic, lifestyle, and environmental factors. Here is a breakdown of the primary causes associated with diverse types of diabetes:

1. Type 1 Diabetes

- **Autoimmune Reaction**: The immune system mistakenly attacks and destroys insulin-producing beta cells in the pancreas, leading to a lack of insulin.
- **Genetic Predisposition**: Family history of type 1 diabetes increases the risk.
- **Environmental Triggers**: Certain viral infections (e.g., Coxsackievirus or Epstein-Barr virus) may trigger the immune response leading to type 1 diabetes.
- **Other Autoimmune Conditions**: People with autoimmune diseases, like thyroid disease or celiac disease, may be at higher risk.

2. Type 2 Diabetes

- **Insulin Resistance**: The body's cells become less responsive to insulin, causing the pancreas to produce more insulin. Over time, the pancreas cannot keep up, leading to elevated blood sugar levels.
- **Genetics**: A strong genetic component exists; family history of type 2 diabetes significantly increases the risk.

- **Obesity**: Excess body fat, especially abdominal fat, contributes to insulin resistance.
- **Physical Inactivity**: Lack of physical activity is associated with increased insulin resistance and obesity.
- **Diet High in Refined Carbohydrates and Sugars**: Diets high in processed foods and sugary beverages increase blood sugar levels and insulin demand.
- **Age**: Risk increases with age as cells become less responsive to insulin.
- **Hormonal Conditions**: Polycystic ovary syndrome (PCOS) and certain endocrine disorders increase the risk of developing type 2 diabetes.

3. Gestational Diabetes

- **Hormonal Changes During Pregnancy**: Pregnancy hormones can block the action of insulin, causing insulin resistance.
- **Obesity and Excess Weight**: Higher body fat levels increase the risk of gestational diabetes.
- **Genetics**: Family history of type 2 diabetes or gestational diabetes increases the risk.
- **Age**: Women over twenty-five are at a higher risk of gestational diabetes.
- **History of Gestational Diabetes**: Women who had gestational diabetes in a previous pregnancy are at increased risk for it in future pregnancies.

4. Other Causes

- **Genetic Mutations**: Certain genetic mutations, such as those causing MODY (maturity-onset diabetes of the young), can impair insulin production or function.
- **Endocrine Disorders**: Conditions like Cushing's syndrome and acromegaly increase insulin resistance.
- **Medications**: Certain medications, including corticosteroids and some antipsychotics, can impair glucose metabolism.
- **Pancreatic Diseases**: Conditions that affect the pancreas, such as pancreatitis or pancreatic cancer, can reduce insulin production.
- **Infections and Viral Illnesses**: Some infections may damage beta cells or trigger autoimmune responses, increasing diabetes risk.

5. Lifestyle and Environmental Factors

- **High-Stress Levels**: Chronic stress may lead to hormonal changes, increasing the risk of type 2 diabetes.
- **Poor Sleep Patterns**: Insufficient or irregular sleep can negatively impact insulin sensitivity.
- **Socioeconomic Factors**: Limited access to nutritious food, healthcare, and education about diabetes management increases diabetes risk.

Summary

While genetics play a role, lifestyle factors, such as diet, exercise, weight, and stress management, are major contributors to type 2 diabetes and gestational diabetes. Type 1 diabetes is more related to genetic and autoimmune factors, though environmental triggers can also contribute. Prevention and management strategies focus on modifiable lifestyle factors and early detection, especially for those with a genetic predisposition.

Annexure 15

Normal Ranges*

Blood Sugar (Blood Glucose Levels)

- **Definition**: Blood sugar level indicates the amount of glucose present in the blood at a specific time.
- **Types**:
  - **Fasting Blood Sugar**: Measured after an 8-hour fast. A normal level is typically below 100 mg/dL.
  - **Postprandial Blood Sugar**: Measured 2 hours after eating. A normal level is typically below 140 mg/dL.
  - **Random Blood Sugar**: Measured at any time, with a general target of below 160 mg/dL for non-diabetic individuals.
- **Importance**: Regular blood sugar measurements show real-time control and help guide daily management decisions. Patterns in these measurements can indicate how lifestyle, diet, and medications affect blood glucose.

HbA1c (Hemoglobin A1c)

- **Definition**: HbA1c is a blood test that reflects the average blood sugar levels over the past 2-3 months by measuring the percentage of hemoglobin bound with glucose.
- **Normal Range**: For most non-diabetic individuals, HbA1c is below 5.7%. For diabetic management, the goal is often below 7%.
- **Significance**:

- **Long-term Indicator**: HbA1c provides insight into long-term glucose control and reduces reliance on individual blood glucose readings.
- **Risk Assessment**: Higher HbA1c levels correlate with an increased risk of complications such as neuropathy, nephropathy, and cardiovascular disease.
- **Goal Setting**: HbA1c is a primary metric used by healthcare providers to evaluate the effectiveness of diabetes management strategies.

- **Limitations**: HbA1c does not capture daily fluctuations and might not be entirely accurate for individuals with conditions affecting red blood cell turnover, like anemia.

*Varies in many studies

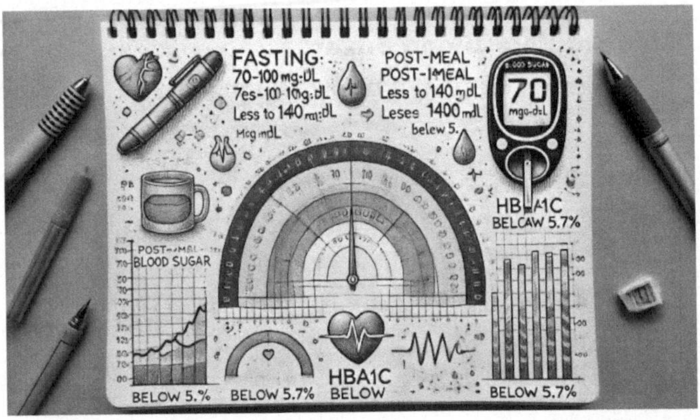

Annexure 16

Insulin levels in different conditions:

Condition/State	Approximate Insulin Level (µIU/mL)	Description
Fasting (Normal)	2 - 20 µIU/mL	Normal fasting insulin levels.
After Meals (Postprandial)	30 - 230 µIU/mL	Insulin spikes after a carbohydrate-rich meal varies based on food and metabolism.
During Exercise (Moderate)	2 - 10 µIU/mL	Physical activity generally lowers insulin levels.
During High-Intensity Exercise	<2 µIU/mL	Intense exercise can significantly reduce insulin levels.
In Obesity	20 - 50 µIU/mL	Higher baseline insulin due to insulin resistance.
In Type 1 Diabetes	Very Low to None	Type 1 diabetes results in incredibly low or absent natural insulin production.
In Type 2 Diabetes (Mild)	10 - 30 µIU/mL	Mild insulin resistance leads to slightly elevated fasting insulin.
In Type 2 Diabetes (Severe)	>50 µIU/mL	Advanced insulin resistance can cause high fasting insulin levels.

Condition/State	Approximate Insulin Level (μIU/mL)	Description
In Pre-Diabetes	10 - 25 μIU/mL	Insulin levels may be elevated as a response to insulin resistance.
Insulin Resistance Syndrome	20 - 70 μIU/mL	Typically, high insulin as the body compensates for reduced effectiveness.
Hypoglycemia (Reactive)	Varies, can be Low or High	Insulin surges can cause blood sugar to drop, leading to reactive hypoglycemia.
Hyperinsulinemia (Excessive Insulin)	>25 μIU/mL	Elevated fasting insulin, often due to insulin resistance or metabolic syndrome.
During Pregnancy	10 - 40 μIU/mL	Insulin may increase due to hormonal changes affecting insulin sensitivity.
Post-Gestational Diabetes	15 - 30 μIU/mL	Elevated insulin levels post-pregnancy in some women; varies individually.
After High-Carb Meal in Insulin Sensitivity	~60-90 μIU/mL	In individuals with good insulin sensitivity, insulin peaks then decreases efficiently.

These values are approximate and can differ based on lab techniques, individual metabolism, and other factors. They provide a general reference for typical insulin levels across various physiological states. For precise information, specific medical tests are recommended.

Annexure 17

Calories Burn during activity

The number of calories burned in different activities depends on factors like body weight, intensity, and duration. Here is an approximate breakdown of calories burned per hour for a person weighing around **155 pounds (70 kg)**. For heavier or lighter individuals, these values will vary.

Low-Intensity Activities

These are activities that require minimal exertion and are often sustainable over prolonged periods.

Activity	Calories Burned (per hour)
Sleeping	50
Sitting (at rest)	75
Light Housework	170
Walking (2 mph)	150
Stretching/Yoga	180

Moderate-Intensity Activities

These require moderate effort, raising the heart rate and can often be sustained for an hour or more.

Activity	Calories Burned (per hour)
Walking (3.5 mph)	280
Dancing (slow)	210
Biking (leisure, <10 mph)	290
Swimming (leisure)	330
Gardening	330
Hiking	430
Golfing (walking, no cart)	330

High-Intensity Activities

These activities involve vigorous effort, significantly raising the heart rate, and can be harder to sustain for extended periods.

Activity	Calories Burned (per hour)
Running (6 mph)	600
Jumping Rope	700
Biking (moderate, 12-14 mph)	600
Swimming (vigorous)	700
Rowing (vigorous)	600
Aerobics (high impact)	480

Activity	Calories Burned (per hour)
CrossFit/Bootcamp	600
Martial Arts	700

Intense Strength Training

Strength training can burn calories, with the added benefit of building muscle, which increases resting metabolism.

Activity	Calories Burned (per hour)
Weightlifting (moderate)	220
Weightlifting (vigorous)	450
Circuit Training	570
Kettlebell Training	600
Rock Climbing	700

Calorie Burn Adjustments

These values are approximate and can be adjusted as follows:

- For a 130-pound (59 kg) person: Subtract about 15%.
- For a 185-pound (84 kg) person: Add about 15-20%.

Tips for Maximizing Calorie Burn

- **Interval Training**: Alternating between high and low intensity burns more calories in a shorter time.
- **Strength and Cardio Mix**: Combining both can improve endurance and metabolic rate.

- **Incorporate Daily Movement**: Adding low-intensity activities, like taking the stairs, increases overall calorie expenditure.

Understanding calorie burn in various activities helps tailor exercise routines for weight management, fitness goals, and overall health improvement.

Annexure 18

Monitoring Sugar level

Continuous Glucose Monitor (CGM) / Glycemic Variability Markers Importance

- **Definition**: Glycemic variability refers to the fluctuations in blood glucose levels throughout the day, including high peaks and low troughs.
- **Markers**:
  - **Standard Deviation (SD)**: Measures how much glucose values fluctuate around the mean glucose level.
  - **Mean Amplitude of Glycemic Excursions (MAGE)**: Indicates the magnitude of blood glucose swings.
  - **Coefficient of Variation (CV)**: Expresses variability as a percentage of the mean glucose.
  - **Time in Range (TIR)**: Indicates the percentage of time blood glucose levels stay within a target range (usually 70-180 mg/dL).
- **Importance:**
  - **Short-Term Control**: Helps capture highs and lows that HbA1c might miss, offering a more detailed view of glucose control.
  - **Quality of Life**: Reducing variability is essential as large fluctuations can lead to symptoms like fatigue, confusion, and increased risk of severe hypoglycemia.

- ○ **Risk Assessment**: High glycemic variability is associated with greater risks of complications, even if HbA1c levels appear controlled.

- **Monitoring**: Continuous glucose monitors (CGMs) are especially valuable for tracking glycemic variability and TIR.

Why Analyzing All Three is Important

Each of these measures offers unique insights into glucose control:

- **Daily control (Blood Sugar)** helps guide immediate adjustments in diet, activity, and medication.
- **Long-term control (HbA1c)** provides a broader view of overall management effectiveness and the risk of complications.
- **Glycemic variability (VGM)** uncovers the risks associated with blood sugar fluctuations, even if average levels seem controlled, and can help reduce the risk of severe hypoglycemia and other adverse events.

Together, these markers provide a comprehensive picture, helping both patients and healthcare providers tailor diabetes management for better outcomes.

Annexure 19

Diabetes effect on Body Organs

Organs commonly affected by diabetes and the associated diseases or complications that can result from poor blood glucose control over time.

Organ/System	Disease/Complication	Description
Heart	Cardiovascular Disease	Increased risk of heart attacks, coronary artery disease, and congestive heart failure.
	Hypertension	High blood pressure due to damaged blood vessels.
	Atherosclerosis	Hardening of the arteries, leading to narrowed blood vessels and reduced blood flow.
Kidneys	Diabetic Nephropathy	Damage to the kidneys' filtering ability, potentially leading to chronic kidney disease or failure.

Organ/System	Disease/Complication	Description
	Proteinuria	Leakage of proteins into urine, indicating kidney damage.
Eyes	Diabetic Retinopathy	Damage to the retina, leading to vision impairment and potential blindness.
	Cataracts	Clouding of the eye's lens, leading to decreased vision.
	Glaucoma	Increased eye pressure causing optic nerve damage and vision loss.
Nervous System	Diabetic Neuropathy	Nerve damage causing pain, tingling, and numbness, often in hands and feet.
	Autonomic Neuropathy	Nerve damage affecting involuntary functions like heart rate, digestion, and bladder control.
Feet and Limbs	Peripheral Arterial Disease (PAD)	Poor blood flow to the extremities, increasing the risk of infections and ulcers.
	Diabetic Foot Ulcers	Open sores and infections on the feet

Organ/System	Disease/Complication	Description
		due to nerve damage and poor circulation.
	Amputation	Severe cases may require amputation due to non-healing wounds or severe infections.
Skin	Diabetic Dermopathy	Brown patches on the skin, often on the shins, caused by changes in blood vessels.
	Necrobiosis Lipoidica Diabeticorum	Yellow or red lesions, often on the shins, due to damaged blood vessels.
	Fungal Infections	Increased risk of fungal infections, especially in warm, moist areas.
	Bacterial Infections	Susceptibility to infections such as boils, styes, and nail infections.
Digestive System	Gastroparesis	Delayed stomach emptying due to nerve damage, causing nausea,

Organ/System	Disease/Complication	Description
		vomiting, and bloating.
	Non-Alcoholic Fatty Liver Disease (NAFLD)	Excess fat buildup in the liver, often linked to obesity and insulin resistance.
Teeth and Gums	Periodontal Disease	Increased risk of gum disease and tooth decay due to high blood sugar levels.
	Gingivitis and Tooth Loss	Inflammation of the gums and potential loss of teeth due to infection and poor gum health.
Brain	Cognitive Decline	Increased risk of dementia and Alzheimer's disease, potentially linked to vascular damage.
	Stroke	Higher risk of strokes due to damaged blood vessels in the brain.
Immune System	Reduced Immune Response	Slower wound healing and increased susceptibility to infections due to

Organ/System	Disease/Complication	Description
		impaired immune function.
Reproductive System	Erectile Dysfunction	Blood vessel and nerve damage leading to issues with blood flow and sensation in men.
	Pregnancy Complications	Increased risk of preeclampsia, preterm birth, and birth defects in women with unmanaged diabetes.

Each organ affected by diabetes can develop specific complications such as high blood sugar damages blood vessels, nerves, and other structures. Proper diabetes management is crucial to prevent these long-term complications and maintain health across all organ systems.

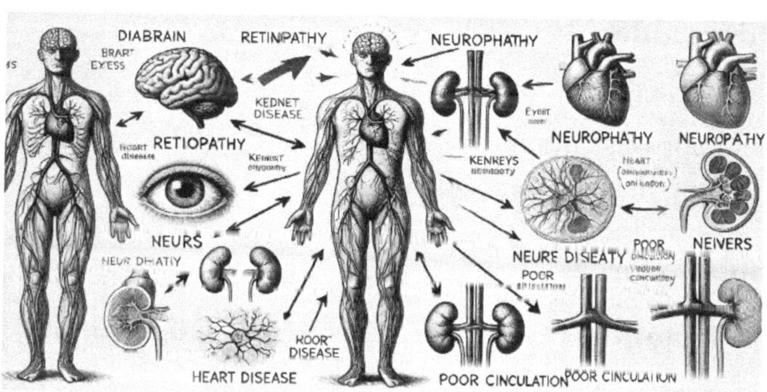

Annexure 20

Commonly used diabetes medications, grouped by their classes and mechanisms of action:

1. Insulin

- **Rapid-Acting Insulin** (e.g., **Lispro, Aspart, Glulisine**): Used before meals to manage blood sugar spikes.
- **Short-Acting Insulin** (e.g., **Regular Insulin**): Manages blood sugar during meals.
- **Intermediate-Acting Insulin** (e.g., **NPH Insulin**): Covers insulin needs for about half a day or overnight.
- **Long-Acting Insulin** (e.g., **Glargine, Detemir**): Provides a steady insulin level throughout the day.
- **Ultra-Long-Acting Insulin** (e.g., **Degludec**): Lasts over 24 hours to stabilize blood sugar levels.

2. Biguanides

- **Metformin**: Reduces glucose production in the liver and improves insulin sensitivity. It is often the first-line treatment for type 2 diabetes.

3. Sulfonylureas

- **Examples: Glipizide, Glyburide, Glimepiride**
- **Action**: Stimulates the pancreas to release more insulin. Commonly used in type 2 diabetes.

4. Meglitinides

- **Examples: Repaglinide, Nateglinide**
- **Action**: Stimulates insulin release but with a shorter duration than sulfonylureas, taken before meals to control postprandial blood sugar.

5. Thiazolidinediones (TZDs)

- **Examples: Pioglitazone, Rosiglitazone**
- **Action:** Improves insulin sensitivity in the body's cells, reducing blood sugar levels.

6. DPP-4 Inhibitors (Dipeptidyl Peptidase-4 Inhibitors)

- **Examples: Sitagliptin, Saxagliptin, Linagliptin, Alogliptin**
- **Action:** Helps increase insulin release and decrease glucose production in the liver by inhibiting the DPP-4 enzyme.

7. GLP-1 Receptor Agonists (Glucagon-Like Peptide-1 Agonists)

- **Examples: Exenatide, Liraglutide, Dulaglutide, Semaglutide**
- **Action:** Mimics GLP-1 hormone, increasing insulin release, slowing gastric emptying, and reducing appetite.

8. SGLT2 Inhibitors (Sodium-Glucose Co-Transporter 2 Inhibitors)

- **Examples: Canagliflozin, Dapagliflozin, Empagliflozin, Ertugliflozin**
- **Action:** Blocks glucose reabsorption in the kidneys, causing excess glucose to be excreted in the urine.

9. Alpha-Glucosidase Inhibitors

- **Examples: Acarbose, Miglitol**
- **Action**: Slows carbohydrate absorption in the intestines, which helps control post-meal blood sugar spikes.

10. Amylin Analogues

- **Example: Pramlintide**
- **Action:** Slows gastric emptying, decreases postprandial glucagon secretion, and reduces appetite. Used in type 1 and type 2 diabetes.

11. Bile Acid Sequestrants

- **Example: Colesevelam**
- **Action:** Lowers blood glucose by mechanisms not entirely understood, possibly affecting cholesterol and glucose metabolism.

12. Dopamine Agonists

- **Example: Bromocriptine**
- **Action:** Improves insulin sensitivity and lowers blood sugar, though it is less commonly used.

These medications are often combined to create a customized treatment plan based on an individual's specific diabetes type, lifestyle, and glucose control needs.

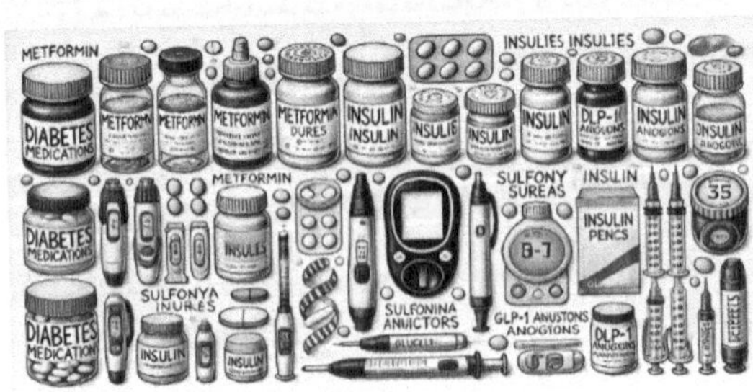

Annexure 21

Non-medicinal treatments for diabetes

1. Dietary Modifications

- **Low-Carb and Balanced Diet**: Limiting carbohydrate intake reduces blood sugar spikes. Emphasis is on whole grains, vegetables, lean proteins, and healthy fats.
- **High-Fiber Foods**: Fiber slows glucose absorption, reducing post-meal blood sugar spikes. Beans, lentils, vegetables, and whole grains are high in fiber.
- **Low Glycemic Index Foods**: Foods like leafy greens, whole grains, and legumes prevent blood sugar surges.
- **Portion Control**: Helps avoid overeating and maintains a steady blood sugar level.
- **Regular Meal Timing**: Eating at consistent times helps regulate blood glucose and prevent dips and spikes.

2. Exercise and Physical Activity

- **Aerobic Exercise**: Activities like walking, jogging, cycling, and swimming improve insulin sensitivity and help maintain healthy blood sugar levels.
- **Strength Training**: Increases muscle mass, which improves glucose uptake and enhances metabolism.
- **High-Intensity Interval Training (HIIT)**: Short bursts of intense activity improve insulin sensitivity.
- **Daily Movement**: Staying active throughout the day (e.g., taking stairs, short walks) prevents blood sugar spikes.

3. Weight Management

- **Weight Loss**: For overweight or obese individuals, losing even a small percentage of body weight can significantly improve blood sugar control and insulin sensitivity.
- **Bariatric Surgery**: For some with severe obesity, bariatric surgery has shown to significantly improve or even reverse type 2 diabetes in many cases.

4. Stress Management

- **Mindfulness and Meditation**: Reduces stress hormones like cortisol, which can raise blood sugar levels.
- **Yoga**: Improves insulin sensitivity and reduces stress levels.
- **Deep Breathing Exercises**: Simple techniques can quickly reduce stress, aiding blood sugar control.
- **Counseling or Therapy**: For those with elevated levels of stress or anxiety, professional support can help reduce emotional stress.

5. Sleep Optimization

- **Consistent Sleep Schedule**: Maintaining a regular sleep pattern improves insulin sensitivity and hormone balance.
- **Good Sleep Hygiene**: A cool, dark, quiet room, avoiding screens before bed, and setting a calming bedtime routine promote quality sleep.
- **Adequate Sleep**: Aiming for 7-8 hours of sleep per night is essential, as poor sleep can raise blood sugar levels.

6. Natural Supplements and Herbal Remedies (with medical supervision)

- **Cinnamon**: Some studies suggest cinnamon can improve insulin sensitivity and lower blood sugar.
- **Berberine**: A compound in certain plants, shown to help regulate blood glucose levels and improve insulin function.
- **Fenugreek**: May improve glucose tolerance and has been traditionally used for blood sugar management.
- **Aloe Vera**: Some evidence suggests aloe vera extract may help in blood sugar control.
- **Bitter Melon**: Known for its hypoglycemic effect and may help reduce blood sugar levels.

7. Alternative Therapies

- **Acupuncture**: May help with pain relief, especially for those with diabetic neuropathy.
- **Biofeedback**: A technique to control physiological processes (like blood glucose) using real-time monitoring of heart rate, muscle tension, etc.
- **Massage Therapy**: Reduces stress and can help with circulation issues common in diabetes.

8. Regular Monitoring

- **Blood Sugar Monitoring**: Tracking blood sugar levels helps to understand the impact of different foods, activities, and stress on blood glucose.
- **Continuous Glucose Monitoring (CGM)**: For those who need frequent monitoring, CGM provides real-time data on blood sugar fluctuations.

- **HbA1c Testing**: Regular HbA1c tests help track average blood sugar over time and gauge overall diabetes control.

9. Hydration

- **Drinking Plenty of Water**: Staying hydrated helps kidneys flush out excess glucose through urine and reduces the risk of hyperglycemia.

10. Education and Support

- **Diabetes Education Programs**: Learning about diabetes management strategies helps individuals make informed lifestyle choices.
- **Support Groups**: Online or in-person groups provide emotional support and practical tips for managing diabetes.

These non-medicinal treatments can be effective, especially for those with prediabetes or type 2 diabetes, in combination with medical advice and monitoring. Lifestyle adjustments are a critical foundation for long-term diabetes management.

Annexure: 22

Exercise Annexure for Diabetic Patients

Introduction

Exercise is an essential part of managing diabetes. It helps to control blood sugar levels, improve insulin sensitivity, and reduce the risk of complications. The American Diabetes Association recommends that adults with diabetes get at least 150 minutes of moderate-intensity aerobic activity or 75 minutes of vigorous-intensity aerobic activity per week. They also recommend strength training at least twice a week.

Types of Exercise

There are many diverse types of exercise that are beneficial for people with diabetes. Some of the best options include:

- **Aerobic exercise:** This type of exercise gets your heart rate up and helps you breathe harder. Examples include walking, jogging, biking, swimming, and dancing.
- **Strength training:** This type of exercise helps to build muscle and improve strength. Examples include lifting weights, using resistance bands, and doing bodyweight exercises.
- **Flexibility exercises:** This type of exercise helps to improve the range of motion and prevent injuries. Examples include yoga, Pilates, and stretching.

Getting Started

If you are new to exercise, start slowly and gradually increase the intensity and duration of your workouts. It is important to listen to your body and not overdo it. If you have any health concerns, talk to your doctor before starting an exercise program.

Safety Tips

- **Check your blood sugar before, during, and after exercise.** This will help you avoid hypoglycemia (low blood sugar).
- **Carry a source of glucose with you in case of hypoglycemia.**
- **Drink plenty of water before, during, and after exercise.**
- **Wear comfortable shoes and clothing.**
- **Exercise in a safe environment.**
- **Listen to your body and do not push yourself too hard.**

Sample Exercise Plan

Here is a sample exercise plan for a beginner:

- **Monday:** 30 minutes of walking
- **Tuesday:** 20 minutes of strength training
- **Wednesday:** Rest
- **Thursday:** 30 minutes of swimming
- **Friday:** 20 minutes of yoga
- **Saturday:** Rest
- **Sunday:** 45 minutes of biking

This is just a sample plan, and you may need to adjust it based on your individual needs and fitness level.

Tips for Staying Motivated

- Find an exercise friend.
- Set realistic goals.
- Make exercise fun.
- Reward yourself for your progress.

Remember:

Exercise is an important part of managing diabetes.

Start slowly and gradually increase the intensity and duration of your workouts.

Listen to your body and do not overdo it.

Talk to your doctor if you have any health concerns.

Annexure: 23

Blood Sugar Tracking Log

Patient Name: ______________________________

Month/Year: ______________________________

Date	Time	Blood Sugar (mg/dL)	Medication (Dosage/ Time)	Meal (Description/ Carb Count)	Exercise (Type/ Duration)	Notes/ Comments

Instructions:

- **Date and Time:** Record the date and time of your blood sugar check.
- **Blood Sugar (mg/dL):** Write down your blood glucose reading from your meter.
- **Medication:** Note the name and dosage of any diabetes medication taken, and the time you took it.
- **Meal:** Briefly describe what you ate and estimate the number of carbohydrates in the meal.
- **Exercise:** Record the type of exercise you did (e.g., walking, swimming, strength training) and how long you did it.
- **Notes/Comments:** Use this space to record anything that might have affected your blood sugar levels, such as stress, illness, lack of sleep, or unusual events.

Tips for Using Your Blood Sugar Log:

- **Be consistent:** Aim to check your blood sugar at the same times each day.
- **Bring your log to your doctor's appointments:** This will help your healthcare provider see patterns and adjust your treatment plan if needed.
- **Look for patterns:** Over time, you may notice trends in your blood sugar levels related to meals, exercise, or medication.
- **Do not get discouraged:** There will be days when your blood sugar is higher or lower than you would like. Use your log to learn and adjust as needed.

This log can be photocopied as many times as needed. You can also create a digital version of this log using a spreadsheet program or a diabetes management app.

Annexure: 24

Wisdom from Diabetes Reversal Champions

This annexure shares insights and practical strategies from individuals who have successfully put their type 2 diabetes into remission. Their experiences offer valuable lessons and motivation for others on the same journey.

1. Prioritize Sustainable Lifestyle Changes

- "It's not a diet; it's a lifestyle change." Many people emphasize that achieving lasting remission requires adopting healthy habits for the long term. Focus on making gradual, sustainable changes to your diet and exercise routine.
- "Find what works for you." There's no one-size-fits-all approach. Experiment with different dietary approaches (e.g., low-carb, Mediterranean, plant-based) and exercise routines to discover what you enjoy and can stick with.

2. Embrace the Power of Food

- "Food is medicine." Many people highlight the importance of whole, unprocessed foods in their diabetes reversal journey. Focus on vegetables, fruits, lean protein, and healthy fats.
- "Cook more often." Preparing meals at home gives you control over ingredients and portion sizes.
- "Read food labels carefully." Be mindful of hidden sugars and unhealthy fats in processed foods.

3. Make Exercise a Habit

- "Find an activity you love." Whether it is walking, dancing, swimming, or gardening, choose activities you enjoy and make them a regular part of your routine.
- "Every bit counts." Even short bursts of activity throughout the day can be effective. Take the stairs, park farther away, or go for a walk during your lunch break.

4. Cultivate a Support System

- "Connect with others." Join a support group, find an online community, or enlist the support of friends and family. Sharing your journey with others can provide motivation and encouragement.
- "Don't be afraid to ask for help." Reach out to your healthcare team, a registered dietitian, or a certified diabetes educator for guidance and support.

5. Focus on Mental and Emotional Well-being

- "Manage stress." Stress can impact blood sugar levels. Find healthy ways to manage stress, such as meditation, yoga, or spending time in nature.
- "Celebrate your successes." Acknowledge your progress and celebrate your achievements along the way.

6. Be Patient and Persistent

- "It takes time." Reversing diabetes is a journey, not a sprint. Be patient with yourself and do not get discouraged by setbacks.
- "Never give up." Believe in your ability to achieve remission and keep moving forward, one step at a time.

Remember: These are personal stories, and individual results may vary. It is crucial to work closely with your healthcare provider to develop a personalized plan for managing your **diabetes.**

Annexure: 25

Glossary of Diabetes-Related Terms

This glossary explains common diabetes-related terms in simple language.

A1C: A blood test that measures your average blood sugar level over the past 2-3 months. It shows how well your diabetes is being managed.

Blood glucose: Another term for blood sugar. It's the main sugar that your body uses for energy.

Carbohydrates: One of the three main nutrients in food (along with protein and fat). Carbs are broken down into glucose, which raises your blood sugar levels.

Diabetes: A condition where your body doesn't make enough insulin or doesn't use insulin properly. Insulin is a hormone that helps glucose get from your blood into your cells for energy.

Fasting blood sugar: Your blood sugar level after you haven't eaten for at least 8 hours (usually first thing in the morning).

Gestational diabetes: A type of diabetes that develops during pregnancy.

Glucagon: A hormone that raises your blood sugar when it gets too low.

Glycemic index (GI): A ranking of how quickly different carbohydrates raise your blood sugar.

Hyperglycemia: High blood sugar.

Hypoglycemia: Low blood sugar.

Insulin: A hormone made by your pancreas that helps your body use sugar for energy. People with type 1 diabetes don't make insulin and need to take it through injections or a pump. People with type 2 diabetes may need to take insulin if other medications aren't enough to control their blood sugar.

Insulin resistance: A condition where your body doesn't respond to insulin properly, leading to high blood sugar. This is a key factor in type 2 diabetes.

Ketones: Chemicals your body makes when there's not enough insulin in your blood. Elevated levels of ketones can be dangerous.

Prediabetes: A condition where your blood sugar is higher than normal, but not high enough to be diagnosed as diabetes.

Type 1 diabetes: An autoimmune disease where your body's immune system attacks and destroys the cells in your pancreas that make insulin.

Type 2 diabetes: A condition where your body doesn't make enough insulin or doesn't use insulin properly. This is the most common type of diabetes.

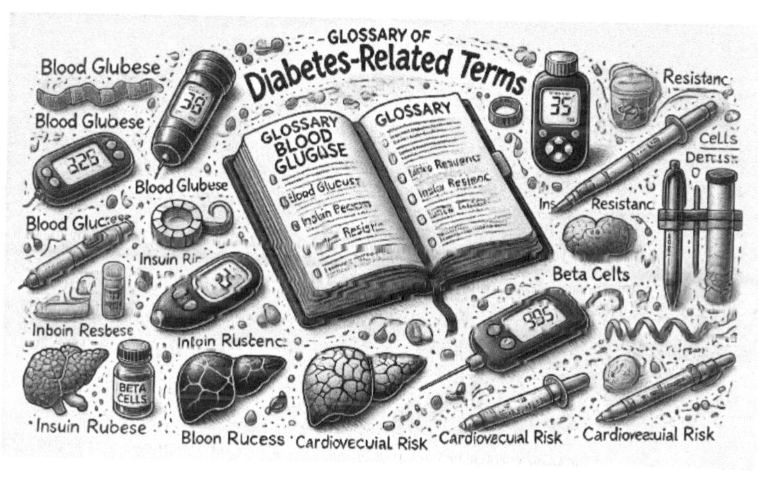

Disclaimer: The book, including the annexures, is for informational purposes only and should not be considered medical advice. Remain under the care of your diabetologist and do not change your medication without consulting him/her. Please consult with your healthcare provider before starting any program mentioned in this book.